The American Dream through the Eyes of Black African Immigrants in Texas

Ami R. Moore

University Press of America,® Inc.
Lanham • Boulder • New York • Toronto • Plymouth, UK

Copyright © 2013 by University Press of America,® Inc.
4501 Forbes Boulevard, Suite 200, Lanham, Maryland 20706
UPA Aquisitions Department (301) 459-3366

10 Thornbury Road, Plymouth PL6 7PP, United Kingdom

Library of Congress Control Number: 2012950809
ISBN: 978-0-7618-6026-6 (cloth : alk. paper)—ISBN: 978-0-7618-6027-3 (electronic)

To all black African immigrants in the world,
your contributions matter. This book is yours.

Contents

Acknowledgments

I wish to thank all of the African-born immigrants who participated in this study. Your lived experiences enlightened my ideas about the book.

Introduction

"…the American dream, that dream of a land in which life should be better and richer and fuller for every man, with opportunity for each according to his ability or achievement. … It is not a dream of motor cars and high wages merely, but a dream of a social order in which each man and each woman shall be able to attain to the fullest stature of which they are innately capable, and be recognized by others for what they are, regardless of the fortuitous circumstances of birth or position"—James Adams (1931, 404).

Adams wrote these words almost eighty years ago in his book, *The Epic of America*. Today, have all Americans achieved the American dream regardless of their fortuitous or unfortuitous circumstances? Do these words still resonate with the experiences of some people in the United States? On November 4th, 2008, the United States of America made history by electing its first nonwhite president whose father was an immigrant from Kenya, East Africa. Does electing a nonwhite—black—president in America mean the American dream is accessible to everyone in the United States?

This research uses Adams' (1931) definition of the "American dream" to examine whether black African immigrants in Texas are achieving the American dream which includes not only the economic aspects of their lives such as material achievement but also a holistic assessment of their lives such as being valued and respected for who they are. Although the concept of the "American dream" pervades American culture, it has most often been used to reflect materialistic ideals such as home ownership (Freeman and Hamilton 2004) and upward mobility goals such as achieving middle class status (Clark 2003). However, another aspect, the moralistic one, such as the ideal of "true regard for the dignity and worth of each and every individual" has been overlooked (Fisher 1973, 161). Thus, using Adams' definition which encompasses both aspects, this book goes beyond merely examining

1

the material accumulation of black African immigrants in the United States. By asking questions such as the ones in the appendix, the study taps into both the material and nonmaterial aspects of the American dream.

A NATION OF IMMIGRANTS WITH DIVERSE EXPERIENCES AND OUTCOMES

From the pioneer founders who were mainly Anglos to its present day immigrants who are mainly non-Anglos and non-Europeans, hundreds of thousands of newcomers have landed on the American shores. They came from all corners of the earth under different circumstances to create the diverse society that we know as the United States of America. Different rationales affect their decisions to migrate. Nevertheless, most immigrants come to the United States to better their lives (Clark 2003). The life experiences and chances of success of each immigrant group vary. As several scholars have indicated, some immigrant groups fare better than others. In fact, they have found that the economic attainment of immigrant workers varies by place of origin and race (Chiswick 1979; Dodoo 1991; Model and Lapido 1996; Model 1997; Poston 1994; Dodoo 1997; Moore and Amey 2002; Kposowa 2002) as well as by gender (Moore, Amey, and Bessa 2009). Further, Bratsberg and Ragan (2000) and Zeng and Xie (2004) both identified host country schooling as the primary factor that explains differentials in economic success among immigrants in the United States.

Studies (Dodoo and Takyi 2002; Moore, Amey, and Bessa 2009) have shown that white African male immigrants earned significantly more than black African male immigrants. Additionally, black African males are disadvantaged in earnings compared to other black workers, including Caribbean black males. They also receive lower monetary returns for education when compared to their Caribbean counterparts (Dodoo 1997). While it is true that most of the blatant, institutional discriminatory practices that held some groups of Americans behind have lessened, some Americans—either native-born or foreign-born—still face cultural, economic, political, and social challenges which hinder their economic progress.

For instance, African Americans have been found to be socioeconomically less successful than white Americans. There is a plethora of scholarly works that have tried to explain why African Americans on average lag behind others, especially white Americans. Some believe that the pervasiveness of past racism and discrimination against African Americans has created structures that led to deep inequalities between whites and non-whites, specifically blacks, inequalities that are still at work today despite all the significant efforts of the civil rights era (Willie 1989; Brown et al. 2003; Benjamin 2005). They argue that black Americans from all socioeconomic classes are victims of such structures regardless of their achievements. Others argue that although there has been a significant change in racial attitudes and treatment of people of color in America, racism still exists and affects non-whites, especially blacks (Bonilla-Silva 2010; Bonilla-Silva and Foreman 2000; Picca and Feagin 2007; Ratansi 2007). These authors believe that some of the contemporary studies in social sciences have not been able to detect the new "kind" of racism because scholars have used the traditional measures of racism which fail to uncover the "new" racism. However, a few scholars have also found that race has become less of an obstacle in non-white Americans' prospects of success. For instance, Wilson (1980) and Sowell (1981) have contended that social class origin is more of a determining factor of economic success than race for blacks in present-day America. Although these scholars recognized the horrendous injustices that black Americans have endured, they believed that changes brought about by the civil rights movement have helped all people of color by improving relations between white and non-white Americans, even black Americans. They believe that the chances of economic success of nonwhite Americans have gotten much better over time.

Another factor that has been examined in the study of minority groups' success has been assimilation. In the United States of America, assimilation means conforming to the Anglo-culture which is the dominant culture established by the English pioneers since the 18th century (Parrillo 2009). In fact, all immigrants that came to the United States after the Anglos, as well as Native Americans, were required to shed their cultural distinctiveness and conform to the Anglo-culture. While, in general, white immigrants found assimilation as a path to social acceptance and economic upward mobility, the lot of non-white native-born Americans and immigrants has been quite different. This has led to criticism of proponents of the traditional assimilation theory which stipulates that immigrants first assimilate to the norms, values, and behavior of the host country and then become accepted into the society (Gordon 1964). Glazer (1993), for instance, questioned the role of the classic assimilation theory since from its inception advocates of this theory excluded native-born nonwhites such as blacks or African Americans. In fact he showed in his article, "Is Assimilation Dead?" how the concept of assimilation is biased against nonwhites and why assimilation has been under attack. Nevertheless, some scholars believe that residential segregation inhibits assimilation into the mainstream culture and reinforces the norms and values of subjugated groups (Hawley 1944; Patterson 2000; Wilson 2009). These scholars usually focus on the struggles of lower class groups such as black Americans in inner cities who are not achieving the American dream, especially the material aspect.

Further, this idea of a linear form of assimilation has also been rejected by some social scientists who have focused on the experiences of immigrants

(Portes and Zhou 1993; Zhou 1997; Waters and Jimenez 2005). For instance, Portes and Zhou (1993) developed the segmented assimilation framework that takes into consideration the fact that immigrant groups bring with them different social and economic backgrounds that affect their chances of assimilating, social acceptance, and success in America. They believe that various forms of assimilation are taking place in the United States and these forms are quite different from the classic assimilation theory that describes the experiences of European immigrants prior to the 1965 changes in the immigration laws in the United States.

As there is no consensus among scholars regarding why some groups in America are still struggling relative to others, using the concept "American dream" as coined by Adams, this book offers another perspective to the debate of whether race is still a factor in the United States. It looks at how black African-born immigrants who have earned an American college degree go through the processes of achieving material goods and whether or not people recognize them for "what they are" instead of "who they are." In addition, it provides insight with regard to how black African-born immigrants navigate the cultural, economic, political, and social environments in America in order to achieve the American dream, not only accumulating material goods but also overcoming other barriers erected because of their race and/or place of birth. The study results can inform policy to combat continued race and ethnic stratification in immigrants' lives. Additionally, black African immigrants have been understudied relative to other groups (Arthur 2000; Obiakor and Grant 2002). This book tries to fill that void. Finally, this book is different from others that have looked at immigrants in the United States because it does not merely focus on the economic success of immigrants, but also on social acceptance and rejection of black African-born immigrants by native-born Americans of all ethnic and racial backgrounds.

METHOD AND DATA COLLECTION

The study used a hermeneutical framework to understand how black African immigrants achieve the American dream because, as stated by Oliver (1983), the function of hermeneutics "is to make clear, reveal, or understand the meaning of texts, language, action and social institutions" (522). This framework allows the author not only to understand the meanings that black immigrants attach to their diverse experiences in the United States, but also their experiences with different American social institutions.

As an African immigrant, the author had a privileged insider perspective that allowed her to apply reflexivity at all times during the research process (Ely et al. 1991). However, being reflective made the author become aware of her own potential biases and preconceptions that may affect what she was trying to understand (Maykut and Morehouse 1994). Consequently, she situated herself in the research and informed prospective participants about her place of origin. She made sure she did not inject any of her personal beliefs in the data collection process and remained as neutral as possible throughout the data collection process. It is important to note that her privileged, insider position created trust between her and the participants. This helped gather information that could be considered sensitive. Furthermore, using hermeneutics, the author was able to assess how black African immigrants interpret their different experiences integrating history, culturally established norms and meanings, as well as contemporary social changes, into their stories (Gadamer 1993).

Data were collected from 80 black African-born Americans in Texas (Dallas, Fort Worth Metroplex and Houston) through the means of snowball sampling from May 2009 to December 2010. The interviews lasted between 25 to 90 minutes. The interviews were conducted in a variety of places at the convenience of the interviewees: in their homes, the author's home, public places such as libraries, bookstores, during association meetings, and in their offices.

A qualitative approach was appropriate for this study because we were interested in knowing the worlds of black African immigrants regarding the American dream. The respondents described their situations, thoughts, feelings, and actions (Taylor and Bogdan 1998) as they reflected on their lives, residing in the United States and interacting within American institutions, from the time they immigrated to the United States until the time of the interviews. Further, in-depth interviews were warranted because we wanted to assess how black African immigrants "make sense of their experiences and construct meanings and selves" as well as deal with the "complexities and subtleties of the social worlds they inhabit" (Chase 2003, 80-81). This approach produced rich, in-depth understandings of black African experiences regarding achieving the American dream.

The study focuses on black African immigrants in Texas (Dallas, Fort Worth Metroplex and Houston) because Texas is among the top five states with the most Africans. Additionally, Dallas and Houston, two important cities in Texas, are ranked among the top 10 American cities with the largest African immigrant populations (Terrazas 2009). Only immigrants from these four African countries—Ethiopia, Ghana, Kenya, and Nigeria—are considered because they are among the four most populous African immigrant groups in Texas according to the 2000 Census data (Table I.1). To be considered, a participant had to have earned a college degree in the United States and be a U.S. citizen. The selection criteria are important for this study because first, to be a U.S. citizen, an immigrant has to live in the country for an extended period of time and thus become familiar with American culture and social institutions. Second, having a U.S. college degree, the immigrant can more likely successfully compete in the market place with native-born Americans. Third, naturalization helps immigrants obtain certain jobs—federal agency jobs, defense industry jobs (Bratsberg, Ragan, Nasir, 2002). Finally, the black African-born Americans who participated in the study have resided in the United States for at least ten years and are employed full time. The 10 years of American residency is necessary because duration of stay is an important factor that affects the socioeconomic status of some African immigrants (Moore and Amey 2002).

THE STUDY SAMPLE

Over half (52%) of respondents were male. The average age of the sample was 51 years of age. Respondents were mostly married (79%). Participants of

Table I.1. African immigrants in Texas by place of origin (Weighted sample).

	Number	Percent
Nigeria	22,239	34.30
South Africa	5,511	8.50
Ethiopia	4,981	7.70
Kenya	4,631	7.10
Egypt	3,712	5.70
Ghana	3,027	4.70
Morocco	1,923	3.00
Liberia	1,729	2.70
Algeria	1,349	2.10
Tanzania	1,213	1.90
Zimbabwe	1,209	1.90
Sierra Leone	1,107	1.70
Cameroon	1,035	1.60
Uganda	673	1.00
Somalia	264	0.40
Senegal	171	0.30
Cape Verde	147	0.20
Africa-not specified	7,766	12.00
TOTAL	64,781	100.00

Source: U.S. Census 2000, PUMS.

this research were all college graduates. Thirteen percent had an associate degree, 47% had a bachelor's degree, 11% had a Master's degree, and 29% had a PhD or an MD. They were in different types of occupations: computer scientists, business administrators, accountants, nurse's aides, educational administrators, nurses, communication professionals, religious leaders, chemists, a surgeon, etc. The mean income was $63,755. Thirty percent earned less than $50,000 a year, 45% earned between $50,000 and $100,000, and 25% earned above $100,000 annually.

This study has some limitations. First, the sample size is small (80 participants). Second, participants are drawn via snowball sampling. Because of the small sample size and the sampling technique, the study findings are limited and may not be generalizable to all African immigrant populations. Third, the study captures the subjective, lived experiences of the African immigrants; hence, their accounts were taken at face-value and no attempts were made to cross-check their reports.

Despite these limitations, this research study is important because not only has it uncovered some of the problematic and challenging experiences that these African immigrants face as non-American native-born, but has also exposed ways they go about surviving in a society that often scrutinizes their identity. It also discusses the paradoxes and contradictions these immigrants face when attempting to develop identification with new cultural and social capital in order to achieve both the materialistic and moralistic aspects of the American dream.

BACKGROUND INFORMATION OF COUNTRIES OF ORIGIN OF PARTICIPANTS

Apart from the transatlantic slavery that brought masses of African immigrants to the Americas, immigration of black Africans to the United States was insignificant until the late twentieth century (Parrillo 2009). Immigration of Africans to the United States became significant after 1965 when immigration laws were massively reformed. The 1965 Immigration and Nationality Act ended the national origin quota system and replaced it with a preference system that put emphasis on immigrants' skills and family relationships (Public Law 1965). Additionally, globalization, economic, and political conditions of African countries, as well as relationships between these African countries and the United States all contribute to the increase in the relatively recent numbers of African immigrants into the United States.

• Ethiopian immigrants: Located in Eastern Africa, Ethiopians are ethnically diverse people. The official language is Amharic. However, Tigrinya, Arabis, Guaragigna, Oromifia, English, and Somali are commonly spoken. With a population of 82 million, Ethiopia is one of the poorest African countries. The estimated GDP per capita for Ethiopia was $365 (2009-2010). Ethiopia has a literacy rate of 43%, and an infant mortality rate of 77 for every 1,000 live births (U.S. Department of State 2011). The median age for Ethiopians is 16.8 years (CIA World Factbook 2011). This means that half of the population is below 16.8 years old and half is above. However, unlike most African countries, Ethiopia has never been under any colonial rule (Hyman, Guruge, and Tizazu, 2008). In general, Ethiopians enjoyed peace and harmony until the mid-1970s when Ethiopia underwent significant challenges that led to the out-migration of its people. In fact, from 1974 onwards, Ethiopia experienced a revolution, wars, and famine which led to a significant exodus of Ethiopians overseas. Since the 1974 revolution, it is estimated that over one million Ethiopians left their native country and some found refuge in the West, including the United States (Hyman, Guruge, and Tizazu, 2008). While Ethiopian migration to the United States could be traced since the 1920s, Ethiopian immigrants entered the United States in significant numbers between the 1950s and 1990s. A point needs to be made here. The United States has historic ties with Ethiopia. Hence, because of these ties, the United States has welcomed more Ethiopians, especially refugees, relative to other African immigrants onto its shores (Gordon 1998). The Ethiopian population in the United States is estimated to be between 250,000 and 350,000 (Getahum 2007).

• Ghanaian immigrants: Ghana is a Western African country with an estimated population of 24 million inhabitants with different ethnic backgrounds. The Republic of Ghana was the first African country to gain independence. Ghana obtained independence from British powers in 1957. The official language in Ghana is English. However, several other languages are commonly spoken: Akan, Mole-Dagbani, Ewe, Ga-Adangbe, Guan, and others (U.S. Department of State 2010). Life expectancy is about 60 years for men and 62 years for women. Sixty-six percent of Ghanaian males and only 50% of Ghanaian females are literate (CIA World Factbook 2011). Ghana has a median age of 21.4 years. Infant mortality rate is estimated at 48.55 per 1,000 live births. The estimated GDP per capita was 2,500 in 2010 (CIA World Factbook 2011). Ghana underwent a series of coups that led to economic and political instability from 1966 to 1979. During this time period, unprecedented numbers of Ghanaians emigrated out of Ghana. Today, it is believed that about 10% of Ghanaians live outside of Ghana (Yeboah 2008). Some of these immigrants are in the United States. Indeed, Ghana is the fifth sending country of African immigrants in the United States in 2007 (Reed and Andrzejewski 2010).

• Kenyan immigrants: The Republic of Kenya is located in East Africa, near the equator. With an estimated current population of 41 million people, Kenya obtained its independence in 1963 from the British. Although a multilingual country, the major languages spoken in Kenya are English and Swahili (BBC News 2011). Half of Kenya's population is younger than 19 years old and half is older than 19 years old. Kenya had a per capita GDP of $770 in 2009. Life expectancy at birth was 60 years for Kenyan women and about 59 for men. Infant mortality is estimated at 52.29 per 1,000 live births (CIA World FactBook 2011). A limited number of Kenyans immigrated into the United States prior to 1970 (Nyamwange, Owusu, and Thiuri, 2001). Also few Kenyans are admitted in the United States as refugees because of the relative peace and stability in Kenya (Odera 2007). However, since the late 1970s significant numbers of Kenyans are immigrating into the United States. In 2004, Kenyans represented the fourth largest African immigrant group admitted in the United States (Odera 2007). Today, it is estimated that 200,000 to 300,000 Kenyan Americans reside in the United States.

• Nigerian immigrants: Nigeria is the most populous African country and is located in West Africa. With an estimated population of 158.2 million people, half of Nigerians are less than 19 years old and half are above 19 years old (BBC News 2011). The estimated life expectancy at birth is at 48 years for the average Nigerian (CIA World FactBook 2011). The per capita GDP was $2,500 in 2010. Infant mortality is about 91.54 deaths for every 1,000 live births (CIA World FactBook 2011). Nigerian immigration to the United States could be traced from the early 1900s when the first wave of Nigerians immigrated to the United States to obtain higher education. However, all of these immigrants returned to Nigeria upon completion of their education (Ogbaa 2003). Later groups of Nigerians who immigrated to the United States from the 1950s onwards began to stay because of changes that occurred in both Nigeria and in the United States. For instance, after Nigeria obtained its independence from Great Britain in 1960, Nigerians were no longer considered British subjects and therefore were not required to obtain a British passport for international travels, including traveling to the United States. Thus, with a Nigerian passport, Nigerians could choose to stay in the United States. Additionally, the Nigerian civil war (1967-1970) and subsequent political and economic instability, and increase in insecurity, led to the immigration of significant Nigerians to the United States (Ogbaa 2003). Presently, Nigeria is the African country with the highest population of immigrants in the United States.

ORGANIZATION OF THE BOOK

Chapter 1, "Pre and post immigration views of black African-born immigrants in Texas," examines the reasons why participants in this study chose to immigrate to the United States (pull and push factors), their perceptions of the United States when they arrived, and their current perceptions. This chapter also explores whether the black Africans considered America as a land of opportunity and the kinds of opportunities that are believed to be available. Although our study participants thought the United States is a land of opportunity and one must work hard to achieve whatever one wants out of life, a few reported that the altruism "America is a land of opportunity" is a trap that gives people a false impression of the United States. The importance of globalization and media portrayal of America in ways that participants viewed the United States prior to their immigration was discussed as well.

Chapter 2, "The American dream as defined by black African immigrants," deals with what black Africans consider their American dream and whether or not they have achieved the dream. Respondents' definitions of the American dream varied and mostly were about the different kinds of opportunity that were available. Also, some of the characteristics used by Hector St. John de Crevecoeur, a renowned immigrant who was the first person to fully explain an immigrant's view of the American dream, were used by respondents. However, most of them reported that they had not personally achieved their American dream. For instance, some had not achieved their personal goals such as owning a business. Others reported external factors such as unfair treatment or discrimination that had slowed their progress. Still others believed that their own shortcomings, such as not having enough time and/or not being focused enough, were the reasons for not accomplishing the dream.

Chapter 3, "Black African immigrants and the American dream as defined by James Truslow Adams," uses Adams' definition of the American dream and analyzes black African immigrants' views with regard to achieving both the materialistic and moralistic aspects of the dream. While most of the study participants reported that their lives have been mostly materialistically improved on one hand, they also shared cases where they have been victims of modern racism on the other hand. Additionally, while the different social institutions (such as the political and educational systems) have all helped participants to better their lives, nonetheless their social lives have been incomplete. This chapter also shows how black immigrants tried to circumvent obstacles that are often erected in their processes of achieving the dream. These findings were explained within the confines of Bourdieu's idea of habitus (1977), challenges of adaptation among immigrants, and the concept of new racism.

Chapter 4, "Migrating out of the United States," discusses black African-born immigrants' views on moving back to Africa or elsewhere. The chapter examines why some immigrants want to return home and while others consider the United States as their home. Most of the participants that reported the desire to migrate out of the United States basically wanted to return to their home countries upon retirement. Several reasons were given, with the low cost of living and the lower pace of life in their native countries as the reasons most given. Additionally, some of the respondents did not want to age in the United States and reside in a nursing home. They believed that residing in an American nursing home would be a sad way to age. Another group of the study participants wanted to return because they felt unaccepted and unwelcome in the United States. Respondents who did not want to migrate out of the United States considered America as their home. They did not want to return to their home countries because all their family members are in the United States. The analysis of the lives of these immigrants was primarily discussed within the concept of transnationalism.

Chapter 5, "Future of American-born children of black African-born immigrants," looks at the views of black African immigrants regarding the future of their American-born children. Participants' views were driven by their own experiences of marginalization in both home and host countries and ethnic identity. Some respondents, especially Ethiopian immigrants, showed a strong sense of ethnic identity which was mainly Afrocentric. Also, almost all of the participants thought that the lives of their American-born children will be much, much better than their own. They believed that the children being born and raised in the United States will fit into American society, thus, will not have some of the cultural and social struggles that respondents experienced.

Chapter 6, "Future of black African immigrants and the American dream," concludes the book by synthesizing the findings presented in this book. Several points are presented. Also, a few questions are raised about the future of black African immigrants in the United States.

Chapter One

Pre and Post Migration Views of Black African-Born Immigrants in Texas

The United States has accepted more non-European immigrants, including African immigrants, since the passage of the 1965 Immigration and Nationality Act, also known as Hart-Cellar Act. This Act abolished the country of origin quota which was advantageous to European migrants and gave precedence to family reunification (Reimers 1992). Since 1965, it is estimated that nine out of ten migrants to the United States were non-Europeans (Keller 2001). Africans, just like other non-European immigrants, have benefitted and are still benefitting from this Act. Although African immigrants represent only 3% of the total immigrant population that has been admitted to the United States, their numbers have grown significantly. There were only 101,520 African-born immigrants in the United States in 1980, but this number drastically increased to 1,023,363 in 2007 (Reed and Andrzejewski 2010). Several factors influence these immigrants' decisions to migrate. In this chapter, the push and pull factors that influenced our study participants' decisions to migrate to the United States will be examined. Also, the views of these black African immigrants about the United States prior to migrating as well as their views at the time of the study will be discussed. Finally, a discussion of whether or not these black African immigrants view the United States of America as a land of opportunity will be presented.

Immigration, the movement of people across international geographic boundaries, has received more attention in recent time because of its magnitude. In fact, more people are living outside their birth places now than ever. For instance, the United Nations reported that the number of people who reside in countries different from their places of birth more than doubled from 1975 to 2000 (United Nations 2002). Several international theories of migration explain the reasons why people decide to leave their home countries and settle in different ones. Like any other group of immigrants, different push and pull factors explain the decisions of black Africans to immigrate into the United States.

Ravenstein (1885; 1889) was a pioneer in the examination of the spatial distribution of migration in his seminal works, "The Laws of Migration." In these articles, he tried to explain migration patterns internally as well as internationally. He identified factors that influenced migration such as distance, population densities, and economic necessities. Later, Lee (1966) revised Ravenstein's work and developed the concepts of push and pull models of migration. Push factors are factors that drive people out of their home countries, while pull factors are factors that draw them to their areas of destination. The push factors, also called the supply factors, may be economic, political, legal, and/or religious factors. The pull factors, also referred to as the demand factors, may be economic, political, religious, social, and/or legal such as changes in immigration laws (Madrigal and Mayadas 2006). In fact, popular and scholarly explanations of migration tend to focus on economic theories as reported by De Haas (2008). While economists focus more on labor market factors, there are social and/or political factors that may force one to immigrate. Also, for some immigrants, there may be a theoretical overlap for their reasons to migrate to the United States.

PUSH AND PULL FACTORS THAT INFLUENCE AFRICAN IMMIGRANTS' DECISIONS TO EMIGRATE TO THE UNITED STATES

The economic determinants of migration are found in the economic theories of international migration such as the neoclassical economics approaches. One of the main tenets of the neoclassical economics models, specifically the macro theory, is that immigration will continue as long as there are wage differentials as well as differences in employment conditions between sending countries and destination countries (Todaro 1969). In fact, immigrants from low-wage countries (a characteristic of most African countries) migrate to high-wage ones (Cadwallader 1992). The high wages offered in countries such as the United States (a pull factor) attract potential immigrants who are pushed out of their native countries because of low wages and unemployment.

The micro theory of neoclassical economics emphasizes the rational choice of individuals who decide to immigrate (Todaro 1969; Todaro and Maruszko 1987; Massey et al. 1993). Migrants expect to earn higher earnings relative to what they would have received in their countries of origin. Indeed, potential migrants engage in a cost-benefit calculation whereby people who migrate tend to believe that the benefits of migrating outweigh the costs, considering a certain time frame (Borjas 1990). From this perspective, immigration is a means through which individuals can maximize their income (Massey et al. 1993). Although these perspectives are popular among economists, only ten percent of the study participants mentioned economic factors as a reason for their migrating to the United States.

The comments below from Joanna, a-35 year old Ghanaian woman who immigrated in 1999 to further her education, reflect participants' sentiments:

> I came to the U.S. in 1999 for school, but I had been here before, like two or three times before I came to school here (US). [...] Before my graduate education, I think at the time it was like an economic boom around the 90s, 1995 was the first time I came to the United States. So I found the country very attractive. And people that had finished school in those days, even though they were immigrants, they had managed to find jobs because the US education, for like the Master's program always focused on internships, and other countries like Canada and the UK did not offer that. So, I wanted something that would give me job experience as well as an education. So, I found the country attractive.

Menni, a business man who migrated in 1997 from Kenya, also came to further his education. At the time, he had a choice between going to Switzerland or to the United States. However, he came to the United States because of some economic opportunity that the United States could offer him. He made the following statements when he was asked why he migrated to the United States:

> Actually, coming to America was my secondary option. My first option was to go to Switzerland. I did apply to some colleges in Switzerland and was accepted. But the choice to come to the United States was based on the fact that I could work and pay my way through college. In Switzerland, the law would not allow me to be a student worker. It meant that my parents would have to pay for everything and by no means could they afford that. So wherever I had to go, I had to make sure that I could work and pay for my education. They just had to give me the stepping stone to get me in there.

It is worthwhile to note that none of the participants stated that they migrated to the United States for economic reasons, such as better prospects for employment. Specifically, none of the study participants mentioned something about "expected long term gains," one of the tenets of the neoclassical economics model.

Additionally, about 60% of the respondents mentioned furthering their education as one of the primary reasons for their immigrating into the United States. However, very few participants (15%) reported that they originally

intended to return to their home countries upon completion of their education. Furthermore, Anglophone immigrants were more likely to find
American education appealing and accessible (a pull factor). The lack of
sufficient universities in their homelands and the fact that only a few native-
born students are admitted each year into these universities (push factors)
prompted some of the participants to look elsewhere for educational opportunities. Madu, a fifty-year old Nigerian male who earned an MBA from Texas
A&M, reported:

> I came to the US to further my education because there was a lot of competi-
> tion in Nigeria for people my age who applied to the universities. A lot of
> competition because there were many people that qualified to attend univer-
> sities, but there were very few established ones. We had only four universities
> at the time.

Kuma, a 42-year old from Ghana, also stated:

> At the time I was living in Ghana, there were only three public universities and
> one private university. It was hard to get into a university even with good
> grades. The universities were not there. The competition was high. But come
> to America and the schools are just there. They are looking for people. That is
> an opportunity and the level of education I have acquired in America, there is
> no way I can get that kind of education in Ghana.

The English language advantage also helps Anglophone students as they look
for colleges and universities in the United States. Africans from English
speaking countries are more represented in the United States as a whole and
among international students who are admitted into U.S. higher education
than their non-English speaking counterparts.

While it is true that economic reasons, such as monetary gains, may
influence decisions to migrate into a different country, other non-economic
factors influenced participants' decisions to migrate to the United States.
However, these decisions were driven by "rational choice," albeit nonmone-
tary ones. Respondents engaged in some cost-and-benefit analysis. At times,
the expected outcomes may not be directly linked to their own lives but their
children's. Mrs. Djoa, a 50-year old female from Ghana who won a lottery
visa and immigrated to the United States with her family in 1987, adequately
described the situation. She had spent some years in England where she
obtained her Bachelor's degree.

> Actually, growing up, some of the kids in Ghana had come over here (United
> States) for their education and in the process some of them have actually come
> back to Ghana. Ok, and when they come back, it seems like they do better than
> those who were left behind. So growing up, all of us had the dream of being
> educated abroad then go back to home (Ghana). So, that was a big thing. And

then, of course, as we grew up, we realize that people our age also have the same dream where they would go educate their children abroad and once they come back to Ghana, they seem to do better in terms of their jobs and salaries that they earn. And that was our dream for our kids, really! So we wanted that kind of education for our children.

Some of the immigrants (35%) migrated to reunite with their family members, especially parents, who immigrated earlier. Family reunification, according to McKay (2003) accounts for two thirds of permanent immigration to the United States each year. Other non-monetary reasons that attracted some respondents in the study were security and peace. A few of the immigrants from Ethiopia and Nigeria were either forced to immigrate or stay in the United States because of wars, social unrest, and/or natural disasters such as drought and famine that took place in their home countries. In fact, the Nigerian civil war, or Nigerian-Biafran war, which began on July 6, 1967, and ended on January 15, 1970, forced three of the respondents from Nigeria to settle in the United States. Some immigrants from Ethiopia also experienced forced migration because of the Ethiopian civil war and/or famine. Due to irregular amounts of rainfall, Ethiopia often experiences drought which causes crop failures and consequently cyclical famines. These have displaced thousands of Ethiopians worldwide. Two of the respondents from Ethiopia fell into the refugee category.

Whether they immigrated voluntarily or experienced a forced migration, almost all of our study participants (95%) came to the United States because they had social networks—established relatives or acquaintances—that were living in the United States. These social networks facilitated their migration decisions and lessened the costs of migration. As suggested by the network theory of migration (Massey et al. 1993), the ties that link migrants in destination countries and potential migrants in countries of origin increase the chances of future migration. These networks include family, kin, friends, and community (Boyd 1989) and are the vehicles through which migration is perpetuated because they reduce the risks and costs of future migration at all levels: financial, emotional, psychological, and social. In general, it is through these networks that prospective migrants learn about the countries of destination. For example, Edward, who used to be a business man and a minister in Ghana, described how friends influenced his migration decision:

Well, I had a lot of friends here (U.S.). In fact, when I was in Ghana, I was doing okay, but when my friends come to visit, they would tell me what was going on here (U.S.). So I was excited. I said, let me came in here (U.S.) and see. In fact, the first time I came, I went back because of the weather. But I came back the second time and then went back. Later, I was coming back and forth because of my business. Eventually, I just said, okay, let me stay for a while.

Folly, a 63-year old from Kenya, also explained:

> My brother came here first, in 1965. When he came back to visit, I convinced
> him to help me come to the United States because everybody wanted to come
> to this country. So he helped me to get an admission to college. And through
> him, I came to America. I stayed with him for a while before I lived on my
> own.

Social network members usually give hope to and create expectations in the
minds of potential migrants. However, once these migrants arrive in their
host countries, their expectations may not always match reality. They may
face unanticipated challenges such as entering into a new culture, learning a
new language, finding work, adapting to a different climate, and so on.
Some, especially children, may be able to adjust rather quickly. Others may
struggle and always think about their home countries. Some may even ro-
manticize about all the good things they left behind.

PRE AND POST-MIGRATION VIEWS OF BLACK AFRICAN IMMIGRANTS ABOUT THE UNITED STATES

International migration is a global phenomenon that affects substantial numbers of people worldwide. This phenomenon usually does not begin over-
night, as decision to migrate is a dynamic process filled with expectations
and dreams. Immigrants generally have great expectations—"the act of looking forward in anticipation of the future" (De Jong 2000, 307). Immigrants
that come to the United States, especially the voluntary immigrants, may
look into the future in anticipation of realizing bright and great futures. They
may hold optimistic views about their journeys and stay because the United
States is the wealthiest country. Consequently, these immigrants may believe
that once they migrate to the United States, they will also achieve some
success. At least they hope that they will be better off migrating to America
rather than remaining in their home countries. They hope to achieve the
American dream.

Several factors help immigrants in their processes of building their
dreams and expectations of migrating to the United States. Globalization, "a
process whereby goods, information, people, money, communication, and
fashion, (and other forms of culture) move across national boundaries" (Eitzen and Zinn 2006, 1) has become pervasive. In fact, the influence of the
mass media and information flows from pioneer migrants have all been considered factors that correlate with one's decision to migrate.

Societies and cultures are becoming increasingly interconnected (Hermans and Kempen 1998). Through this interconnection, people and cultures
that traditionally were unaware of the cultures and lives of Westerners are

now exposed to these realities. Different media outlets facilitate this exposure (Appadurai 1990; Deaux 2006) and make living in these societies appealing to potential migrants. These means of mass communication tend to glamorize life in the United States and create inaccurate representations in the minds and hearts of their audience. This creates some unrealistic expectations in the minds of potential migrants, especially the younger ones. At times, when these migrants arrive in the United States, they experience great culture shock. However, the majority tends to overcome these issues as time passes (Cerase 1974). Others may struggle at different degrees to adjust to the culture of their host countries.

Respondents fell into two groups with regard to their pre-migration views of the United States. Participants who immigrated when they were young had more fantasized views; while those who migrated when they were older (at least 30 years old) had more or less realistic views. Some of the recurrent themes that respondents used to describe their pre-migration feelings, attitudes, and views toward coming to the United States were all positive and cheerful, such as "joy," "excitement," "content," and "great."

Imani, a 36-year old Ethiopian woman who immigrated at the age of sixteen, explained her pre-migration feelings and views of the United States:

> I was excited, I was sixteen. Who did not want to come to America at that age? ... You get the excitement. You are going to have everything you want, clothes, TV, and so on. You watch all the shows about America and you think you will have a chance to live some of it.

Fred, a 63 year-old from Ghana who migrated when he was 27 years old, stated, "When I was back home, I thought coming here was like being in heaven. You think of all the good things that you can secure. Your imagination goes wild."

Abasi, a 47-year old man from Kenya, who immigrated when he was 32 years old for educational purposes described his pre-migration views and sentiments below:

> Although I was happy to secure a visa for the United States, I knew that America is not a land of milk and honey where anyone can easily get these. Also, I knew that there are racial issues and I planned to stay to myself as much as possible. I was happy that I received a graduate scholarship. I admire the United States for granting scholarships to people anywhere in the world to come and study.

Additionally, potential migrants obtain information from pioneer migrants who are basically their social networks. However, evidence suggests that information flows between early migrants and potential migrants are often inaccurate. Pioneer migrants may exaggerate positive experiences while underplaying the negative ones (Howenstine 1996; Sladkova 2007; Mahler 1995; Pessar 1995).

As stated earlier, once migrants arrive and settle in the United States, their expectations may seem unrealistic. Respondents reflected on how they found life in the United States upon arrival. All the participants reported that life in America was difficult and challenging in different ways. Some reflected on the different kinds of help that they were able to obtain back in their home countries, while in the United States they now have to do everything themselves. Mandele simply put it as follows:

> Back home, like when I was back home, for example, I have people like a person who does a lot of things for me. Like for example one who drives me and then my wife has about two people who are maids too, [...]. It is not like here. You have to do everything for yourself.

To explain his points he then proceeded with this example:

> Recently, some couple came just about four months ago. And the lady was saying that she gets up like early every day. She goes to work at 5:30 in the morning. Then I asked her what time does she get up. And she said that she gets up like 4:30. I then asked her what time did she get up in Ghana. Her husband responded for her that she got up anytime that she wants, but here she is forced to wake up at 4:30 a.m. So that is the difference.

Another respondent, Mutoni, migrated to the United States in 1992 in his early twenties. He explained how life was easy for him in Kenya relative to the United States:

> At my age, we were not required to work back in Africa. You can stay with your parents and don't have to work no matter what age you are. As long as you are under their roof, they provide for you. Life was easy. We did not struggle.

Some even wanted to return to their home countries as stated by Afaafa from Ethiopia who came to join her mother.

> When I first came here, what I saw was different from what I was used to. Back home, we always think that coming to America is like going to heaven. However, you have to work hard to move from point A to point B. I wanted to go back home, it was too hard for me.

There were other issues that made life uneasy for respondents when they first arrived in the United States. Some talked about difficulties with the culture, discrimination, and people not being able to understand them because of their accent. Dawit, a 22-year old who migrated from Ethiopia when he was eight years old, recounted:

> It was difficult, language barrier and everything. I had to repeat third grade because I could not speak the language. I had no clue, I was just culture shocked. I was young and I think it was more difficult for me even though I adjusted fast. But it was a major change, you know. For older people, they can analyze and be like, okay, it's a new culture. For a kid though, it's like wow! Never knew it was like this, you know. It's like a whole different planet. You get into it and you are confused for a while. But, I guess, you pick up things faster since you are a kid. You soak in things easily.

Dawit later discussed another difficult experience that impacted him for life. He explained:

> When I was a little kid, I lived in a predominantly white community. And right when we came to this community, I befriended this Indian kid. And he took me to his house. His mom asked me where I was from and I told her I was from Ethiopia. And she made this comment: 'oh you guys came to America for food?' […] I wish I could meet her now, you know. It's just stuff like that, as a kid, you hold onto that and you want to prove everybody wrong by achieving in school and being successful in life.

Other respondents talked about the weather being too cold for them. While at the time of the interviews most of the participants stated that they had adjusted to the American life and had somewhat gotten used to some of the challenges, others (37%) still had difficulties fully assimilating into the American culture especially. For instance, Laura, a 35-year old from Ghana who had been in the United States for eleven years, explained her difficulty interacting with American-born because of the different cultural expectations:

> Because of the way we are brought up, we are always upfront with people. We are not pretentious. But here, I feel you have to pretend to a point to get along with people and get things done, or else, if you speak your mind, as a black person, it is always associated with aggression. […] Here, I find myself making sure that whatever I say I have rehearsed it in my head a couple of times and make sure that it comes out right. I analyze the possible implications before I go forward and say something.

Some of these difficulties will be examined in the next chapters along with ways that these immigrants try to overcome them. Although respondents found life in the United States difficult and challenging, at the same time most of them considered the United States as a land of opportunity, especially with regard to acquisition of material goods.

THE UNITED STATES OF AMERICA, A LAND OF OPPORTUNITY

Different reasons were given to explain why the United States is a land of opportunity. Some respondents evoked the American exceptionalist character. American exceptionalism, as defined by Shafer (1999, 446), is "the notion that the United States was born in, and continues to embody, qualitative differences from other nations." It is believed that this unique American quality is what draws countless numbers of immigrants to these shores. While some immigrants talked about America being a land of opportunity by comparing it to their home countries, and even at times to the world, others compared it to other Western countries that they had lived in prior to migrating to the United States. The overarching theme was the opportunity to further education if one chooses to do so. In fact, a substantial number (65%) of respondents believed that education is the key to success. Agatha, a 48-year old registered nurse, shared her belief:

> Compared to Nigeria, there are so many opportunities here (United States). If you want to go to school, you have the opportunity to get grants or loans, and so many other things. You can work and go to school at the same time. Here, you can even get pregnant and still go to school.

Moussa believed that no place on earth matches America relative to the opportunities that it offers to immigrants. He explained:

> Well, America has so many opportunities that you cannot find in another place on earth, you know. If you cannot make it here, there is no way you can make it anywhere else. [...] Here, you are given more chance, you know, to advance yourself. For instance, here as an adult, you can even go to school, but in Africa, it is difficult to do so, you know.

Emmanuel, an industrial engineer who had lived in the United Kingdom before immigrating to the United States, stated:

> I think there are a lot of opportunities here (United States). There is no limitation here on what you wanna do, provided that you are forceful and set forth to do it. I think the sky is the limit and you can go a long way.

The least mentioned reason was freedom to do whatever pleases one as long as it is legal. Five percent of participants reported that in America one is free to do, act, or say anything that one considers important. Olubami, a 54 year old Nigerian professor with a doctoral degree in Technology and Distance learning, shared his reasons:

> One time I opened a sewing factory in here (United States), bought used sewing machines and made them work again. I was making great money

sewing clothes. I was making women's blouses, men's shorts. But being an academician, you see, that is not the kind of job for somebody who is very educated. If I only had a high school degree, or was in middle school, I would have made a career out of that. [...] I did it here. But, I would not be found sewing in Nigeria. I would never have wanted somebody to see me on a sewing machine. But here, I could do it. [...] Even back in Nigeria, my mother was not happy when she learned that I was sewing in America. That was embarrassing to her. However, I made good money. With all my degrees, I never bought a brand new car. It was from sewing, which is supposed to be a lowly job, that I bought a brand new car for the first time. So, there is a difference here. I can do anything that I want here, but I cannot do the same thing in Nigeria. This is why I believe America is a land of opportunity.

It is worthwhile to note that although black African immigrants that we interviewed considered the United States as a land of opportunity, they also reported that one has to work hard in order to achieve something. They were not naïve in their beliefs that anybody who migrates to the United States may merely achieve without any effort. The common phrases that were used to express this sentiment were "nothing is handed to you," "you have to work hard to achieve your goals." For instance, Theo explained, "If you come to this country and you are a very hard worker and want to move forward, then you can achieve." Tariq also explained as follows, "Oh definitely, America is a land of opportunity. If you want to take advantage of it, then you can achieve something. Not that you just sit around, you know." Owusua also stated, "Yes, I perceive America as a land of opportunity, but the opportunity avails itself to individuals who have identified that opportunity and have answered the questions what do I need to do to take advantage of the opportunity."

The American exceptionalist supposition is ubiquitous. It is presented by both politicians and non-politicians alike. In fact, this notion of American exceptionalism is the core of the definition of the American dream by James Adams (1931). One of the general premises of American exceptionalism is that America is a land of opportunity for all where hard work usually leads to material success (Jillson 2004). Although some Americans as well as non-Americans question the validity of the American dream, the concept has been evoked and reiterated in different arenas as if to convince doubters that this concept is real and effective in peoples' lives. For instance, the 2004 Democratic and Republican convention speeches of then-Illinois Senator Obama and California Governor Arnold Schwarzenegger (Elahi and Cos 2005), as well as the 2007 commencement speech of Martin C. Jischke (2007), all reinvigorated the immigrant dream and the quintessential outcome of the America dream. Nevertheless, a few respondents (7%) had some reservations regarding the truism America is the land of opportunity or American exceptionalism. They may be among those Americans who question this notion. For instance, Akosua did not mince her words when she explained:

> Yes and no, America is a land of opportunity. This place, if you can, if you have a vision and if you have patience, you can make it better here than Africa. You know, a lot of people that I have known did good in Ghana too. The 'no' part is that here you work long hours, you get paid and the money is gone right away. You pay nothing but bills. It is a trap. You will be trapped. I don't care what profession you are in. You will be working and paying your bills until! [an expression to mean forever].

Akosua's comments convey the notions of consumerism and work excess, traits that have been used by scholars to describe American society. For instance, Schor (1992), in her book *Overworked American*, documents how American society has adopted a work and spend ideology as a way of life. Others have even examined consumerism and excess work from a religious perspective to rein in and remind people of different faiths of the un-authenticity of this philosophy and its harms to family, community, and society as a whole (Himes 2007). Indeed, some black African immigrants have become a part of this ideology of consumerism and excess work as well.

SUMMARY

The focus of this chapter was to examine the push and pull factors that prompted black Africans to immigrate into the United States and gauge their pre and post-migration views of the United States and their views with regard to the truism America is a land of opportunity. Findings indicate that these immigrants migrated to the United States because of economic, political, and social factors in their home countries. Also, rational choice guided their decisions to migrate even though some of these decisions were not economically motivated. Additionally, while participants who immigrated when they were young tended to have unrealistic representations of the United States prior to their migrating, older ones had less fantasized views of the United States of America. Most of the participants had difficulties with American life when they first arrived in the United States, but some were able to overcome these as time progressed. Others still had problems with some of the cultural expectations. However, the study participants found America as a land of opportunity because of the diverse opportunities and options that America offers to its inhabitants. Nevertheless, a few believed that the truism "America is a land of opportunity" may be just a cliché since in reality the opportunities have strings attached to them.

Although this sample is unique in the sense that only people who had received a higher education in the United States were studied, future research may examine the coping mechanisms of black African immigrants when they arrive in the United States. Questions such as: who stays, who returns, how long does it take for immigrants to give up the thoughts of returning to Africa, and what factors affect their decisions to stay in the United States may enlighten not only immigration scholars, but help prepare and comfort immigrants that find American life too difficult to withstand, thus easing their stress. These immigrants will know that they are not the only ones who have a desire to return to their home countries. Also, they will be able to apply some of the coping mechanisms that worked for others and help them endure their stressors. Finally, it is important that immigrant children that come from low-income countries, especially countries in which English is not a national language, go through some cultural immersion program whereby they are gradually exposed to the American culture. This way, they are not directly thrown into American society where they would have no clue with regard to how to behave and express themselves. Migration being a stressful experience, any program that will lessen the pain and suffering of children should be welcomed.

Chapter Two

The American Dream as Defined by Black African Immigrants

The American dream is a phrase that is embedded in American society. It is commonly used in economic, social, political, and cultural settings. Also, there are hundreds of books and articles written about this concept. Although it means different things to different people, for the average American it represents a possibility of success, especially an economic success, measured, in general, by an upward mobility. The American dream is about possibilities afforded to one to be able to achieve the necessary resources in order to move upwardly in society (McClelland and Tobin, 2010). The tangible measures of the American dream are material possessions such as owning a home. It also connotes political freedom (Clark 2003). However, James Adams' (1931) definition of the phrase, American dream, focused mainly on two areas: materialistic and moralistic ideals. The materialistic aspect defines material accumulation, while the moralistic ideal connotes the idea that all human beings should be equally treated with no regard to their ascribed characteristics such as one's family of origin, place of birth, race, etc.

This chapter examines what African immigrants consider their American dream from the materialistic characteristic especially. It also examines whether or not our study participants believe they had achieved the American dream. Additionally, it analyzes hindrances that these immigrants encountered while trying to achieve their American dream. However, the chapter first begins with a brief overview of the history of the concept "American dream." Although historians would have a lengthy presentation of circumstances in which the concept of American dream was used or envisioned, along with names of people who were significant actors in these events, we have selected just a few instances in which the American dream was typified. This is so because this chapter is not about the history or a repertoire of relevant instances where American dream concept was used, but it is mainly about the American dream as defined by black African immigrants in Texas who participated in our study.

The notion of the American dream is believed to have been part of American history since the beginning of the creation of the United States (Cullen 2003; Jillson, 2004). Not only does it mean different things to different people, but also it means different things at different times. Nonetheless, it is important to note that the phrase "American dream" was not exactly used in some of the instances, and, in other cases, the visions of the people at the time reflected this concept instead. For example, in the early 1600s, the Puritans who came to America wanted to create a different society than the one they emigrated from in England. Thus religious freedom was their American dream (Cullen 2003). In fact, because of their religious faith, the Puritans always reminded each other to keep their focus on God as they believed that the New World was a blessing to their dream (Jillson 2004).

Another era that has frequently been discussed with regard to the American dream was the action of the founding fathers in the late 1700s in charting the Constitution. The founding fathers' visions of America are captured in the Declaration of Independence. Their American dream was encapsulated in the rights that are given to Americans: Life, Liberty, and the Pursuit of Happiness (Cullen 2003; Jillson 2004). However, as these rights have not and are still not equally granted to all Americans, some groups have fought and are still fighting for their American dream of equal rights. People who have been disenfranchised such as racial and/or ethnic minority groups have hoped and are still hoping that America will offer them better opportunities in order to improve their chances of achieving the dream in both its materialistic and moralistic ideals.

Some political figures as well as civil rights leaders have spoken and fought for all Americans to achieve the dream. One of such peoples was Dr. Martin Luther King who made the famous speech "I have a dream," which was a dream of equality among all people regardless of their ascribed statuses in the United States of America as well as in the world. Today, America has undergone significant changes and equality among different groups has been relatively achieved. Native-born as well as foreign-born Americans are supposedly to have no substantial barriers to achieving the American dream. What is the American dream for black African immigrants? Have these immigrants achieved the dream? Before answering these questions, let us take a look at a renowned immigrant, Hector St. John de Crevecoeur, who was the first person to fully explain an immigrant's view of the American dream (Jillson 2004:56).

In his book, *Letters from an American farmer,* Crevecoeur (1782) used some unambiguous words and phrases to convey important characteristics of America that described the American dream and the opportunities that were available to immigrants. He described the United States as a place where "man is free as he ought to be" (50), and as for the meritocratic system that rewarded people according to their efforts, "Here the rewards of his industry follow with equal steps the progress of his labour..." (55). Crevecoeur later talked about how America helped good people achieve an upward mobility: "If he is a good man, he forms schemes of future prosperity, he proposes to educate his children better than he has been educated himself; ..." (79). However, he also warned potential migrants that America is not for everyone, and that only people with certain traits become successful: "It is not every emigrant who succeeds; no, it is only the sober, the honest, and industrious: ..." (80). Crevecoeur's writings were over two centuries ago. What is the American dream for black Africans in this third millennium America?

The following sections examine our study participants' definitions of the American dream. Participants' descriptions of the American dream varied. Some respondents even mentioned that there is no one single dream, but dreams. However, several concepts conveyed the ideas of resource availability such as: opportunities, amenities, rewards for one's work (meritocracy), safety, security, and freedom. Additionally, opportunities and freedom have some overlapping characteristics such as jobs and education, as shown in the Venn diagram in Figure 2.1.

DEFINITION OF THE AMERICAN DREAM: INTERSECTION OF OPPORTUNITIES AND FREEDOM

Participants' definitions of the American dream mostly (86%) focused on the availability of different kinds of opportunities. These opportunities have been identified as the reasons why America has been and is still attractive to immigrants (Borjas 1999; Clark 2003; Massey 1999; McWilliams 1973; Miele 1920). Specifically, for some of the black African immigrants, their definitions of the American dream were availability of jobs, but also the freedom to have whatever job that one wants provided that one has the required qualifications. Also, they reported that with the availability of jobs and freedom, one is able to acquire material objects such as a home in any neighborhood one can afford. The following comments explain the points.

Beheilu, a 60-year old Ethiopian man who immigrated at the age of 26 and had a doctoral degree in business administration, explained:

> The American dream for me is opportunities. Opportunities and freedom to own a house when you want and where you want. Uh, it is freedom to get a job where you want and when you want it, what you are qualified for and then be free to do what you need to do. That is what I think the American dream is associated with, freedom to ownership of land and property, economic opportunities. That's it!

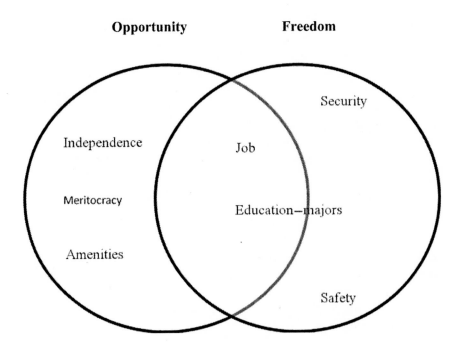

Figure 2.1.   Venn diagram of the definitions of American dream.

Richard, a 47-year old man from Nigeria, explains his definition of the American dream by touching on both the economic aspect and social justice:

> The American dream, for me, is being able to get the position that you have been prepared for, you are qualified for, and you can get it, and you do get it. A job that you know you are doing because of what you have put into it. And once you get it, you see the fruit of your labor, the compensation, the remuneration should equal the job that you are doing. With that in mind, you could have the freedom to do whatever you want without breaking the law. You would not be afraid of the police if you are driving in the wrong neighborhood, not being afraid of being stopped.

It may be worthwhile to note that these ideas of the American dream may just be ideals as it will be shown in the next chapter participants reported some difficulties realizing their dream because of personal and external factors. Some respondents also mentioned the ability to care for one's family as something important in their definition of the American dream. Joanna simply stated, "The American dream is owning a house and making sure that you are able to care for your family by having a good job." Agatha commented as follows, "Back home, my dream was family, job, and marriage. These work quite well in America because as long as you have a job to support your family that is the American dream. In other countries, you will have a family but not a job to support them, so things don't work out. But here, you can have a job that allows you to support your family."

Other themes that intersect are the opportunity to get an education and the freedom to choose whatever field in which one wants to major. Almost half of the respondents (47%) mentioned both education and the availability of resources, such as loans for people who cannot afford to pay, as their American dream. Also, the way the American higher education is set up is the American dream for some. They were able to further their education once they migrated to the United States as adults, an opportunity that they would not find and/or is difficult to achieve in their native countries. Celine, a 47 year old registered nurse who migrated at the age of 27, stated:

> In America, everybody has opportunity to grab good things in life. The American dream means everybody should have at least an average standard of living. They make available the opportunities for people to go back to school so that you can be at least comfortable in life. [...] In Nigeria, the government does not support us, and we had to do everything on our own. But in America, if you want to go back to school, the government will support you. You can even get loans to study here. Going to school here is no big deal, but in Nigeria it is difficult. The sky is the limit here. I can again go back to school and study whatever I want.

Some described a plethora of majors in American higher education as their American dream, and students can freely select whatever field they want to major in and may freely change their minds and change majors when needed. Abeba, a 42-year old from Ethiopia, explained:

> In my country, the educational system does not allow you to choose your major. It depends on your grades. You know the SAT test that they have here, there is something similar in my country. So the major that you are in depends on your grades. But here, you can change your major ten times if you want to. That is really good. [...] I am currently getting an education. Probably I would not have qualified for this major that I am doing right now if it was in my country. I would be in a different major which I would not even enjoy. But now I get to choose what I want to do.

Yemisi from Nigeria also commented, "Here, you can choose and change your major as much as you want. You don't have to be stuck because of your financial situation. [...] There are loans and financial aid."

Contrary to the United States, higher education in Africa is very competitive and only a select few are admitted into the few available colleges and universities. Despite the growing numbers of students each year, access is still severely restricted (Teferra and Albachi, 2004; The World Bank 2010). In fact some of the participants alluded to this problem (which was mentioned earlier in chapter 2) and credited America for being the place where they were able to obtain some of the things they would never obtain or would obtain with greater difficulty in their home countries, such as getting a higher education. Thomas, a 56-year old man from Kenya who received a scholarship to attend college in the United States, shared, "America made me what I am today. I will not be what I am today if I was in my country; education would have been a problem. I will not have a master's degree in business administration."

It is noteworthy to report that respondents in this study were not the first to appreciate the American higher educational system and its opportunities. Brint and Karabel (1989) discussed how the American educational system is open and democratic. Unlike the educational systems in other high-income countries, the American system avoids early selection or tracking. This gives not just one chance to succeed academically, but several chances to students who do not have great academic records. It allows one to achieve upward mobility as long as one is determined to complete the academic requirements. However, it is also important to note that adult immigrants tend to have greater difficulties accessing and succeeding in higher education than native-born Americans. They also have, in general, a lower educational attainment. Nevertheless, naturalized citizens are more likely to have at least a bachelor's degree compared to the overall American population (Erisman and Looney, 2007). Our study participants are among the naturalized citizens and probably represent the elite group of people who, despite the challenges, are able to successfully earn their American higher education degrees.

DEFINITION OF THE AMERICAN DREAM: THE OTHER THEMES

Another common theme used by our study participants in describing their American dream was independence. This theme was mostly used by younger respondents—10% of respondents—who were less than 30 years old. America offers them an opportunity to become economically and socially independent from their parents. They were able to work, go to school, have their own apartment, and vehicle, without relying on anyone for support. Yenee, a 25-year old from Ethiopia, commented:

> To me, the American dream is just being successful, being independent, successful as in just supporting yourself without family help. Like where I am from, people live together, not just your family, but your uncles and aunties live with you. I mean I do not think they want to live that way. It's just that they have to live together in order to support each other. Over here, you can have two or three jobs and you can have your own place. So the American dream to me is just being independent and happy. That might be a little hard if you are working three jobs, but having my own place, supporting myself

without anybody's help is being successful and having an education of course! That helps a lot.

Some of the things the average American takes for granted are part of what constitutes the American dream for some of the study participants. About 35% of respondents referred to amenities that the United States offers which are lacking in their home countries. Some mentioned infrastructure such as good roads, and reliable provision of electricity and water. Menni stated, "Obviously, I can get hot water any time I want. The lights don't go out in the middle of the meal. The roads are in good condition. I have been able to raise my children in a good environment."

Others discussed the opportunity for exceptional medical technology and health education that are available in the United States. Kathrine, a 56-year old licensed vocational nurse, explained, "I would say the American dream is that health wise, you have it. They have the technology to take care of you when you are sick." Mrs Djoa also recounted, "Here they have health literacy. I know back in Ghana, we believe that the fatter you are, the healthier you are. But, I have learned from living here that this is not good. Of course, things are changing in Ghana too."

Still others discussed security and ways that law enforcement officials reinforce the law as their American dream. These give them freedom to live and go about their activities with no worries. Darweshi, a 56-year old who migrated from Kenya at the age of 20, explained:

> I feel more secure being here than over there. You know the things that have been happening there. Like people breaking into homes. So I feel more comfortable, free being here than over there. [...] Yes, security! You can go out and have a good time at night here, but if you do that back home, you never know if you can get back alive. So there is good security here.

Ife also shared,

> I am free here. I do not have to be scared like in Nigeria. In Nigeria, people can come to your house and steal your things. And even if you call the police, they may not be able to do anything. Not even when somebody is being beaten. But here, I am sure, if a police sees someone being beaten, they will come for help. There is more security here.

Overall, participants also reiterated some of the points made by Crevecoeur. They believed that the available opportunities were not for everyone, but for the willing. Afolabi, a 64 year old from Nigeria, stated, "I would define the American dream as opportunity for the willing. Those who are willing to tap into what is available will be successful." Yenee, a 36-year old lady from Ethiopia, shared: "To me, American dream is about the opportunity. If you really want to do something with your life, this is the place to be." Abasi from Kenya also recounted:

> American dream is an opportunity to be who you can be. It is an opportunity to realize one's dream. If you have dreams, then you have to make pragmatic decisions to achieve them. I have seen people who come here and succeed. And I have seen people who come here and fail. These people would have been better off had they never come to America.

Additionally, like Crevecoeur, respondents believe in meritocracy, and they also mentioned that in order for the dream to materialize, one has to make it happen through hard work and determination. Mrs Djoa's comments demonstrate the point when she was asked how she would define the American dream:

> Basically, from my own perspective, the American dream would be to live a life that rewards your effort. This society actually is where your effort, in trying to make yourself a better person in preparation for the future, is recognized. So the American dream yes, you've made the effort, the reward comes, and you enjoy them. The society has, the American society has the necessary ingredients to help you get your full potential. And if you use it, you should get reward. That's the American dream.

Mrs. Djoa was later asked what she meant by "necessary ingredients" and she stated that these are opportunities and resources that America offers. Furthermore, Clara, a 43 year old mother of two who migrated from Kenya, defined the American dream below:

> Well, I can say it is what individuals can do. You can be very independent and you can do anything you want. You can reach your dream. If you want to be a doctor, you can be a doctor. If you want to be a pilot, you can be a pilot. If you want to do something and you have the determination, you can do whatever you want.

Furthermore, as described by Crevecoeur, some respondents mentioned the importance of giving their children a chance to get a better education and a better life than themselves as their American dream. Edem, a 33 year-old old man from Ghana who had a bachelor's of Science degree in chemistry, said: "I see the American dream as success for my family. I want my kids to grow up and be better than who I am in terms of life and education." Zoputa, a 48-year old registered nurse from Nigeria, also shared:

> For me, the American dream means making my children's lives better. Their lives should be better than mine. They should be able to get everything they need without sweating and suffering too much. Especially the girls should

have better education and jobs so no man can mess with them and ask them to leave their house. I think here, you can get everything if you work hard.

Zoputa's comments, especially her emphasis on the importance of girls getting "better education and jobs so no man will mess with them and ask them to leave the house" reflects an aspect of gender inequality. In African societies, since most men are more educated than women and hence economically well off, men do not hesitate to ask their spouses and girlfriends to leave their house in case they no longer see eye to eye. Also, unlike in Western societies where the distribution of couple's property is negotiated via the judicial system, it is not unusual in Africa for men to just sack the women from the family house.

In general, respondents' definitions of the American dream mostly covered material possessions or possibilities to achieve material goods. However, about 12% of the study participants had an issue with the concept. One of the respondents, Osaze, a 75-year old retired surgeon from Nigeria, even went as far as referring to the American dream as an "American nightmare." He confided:

> [...] It is not the American dream, it is the American nightmare. The concept of the American dream is okay that you have your own house, you have a car, you have this and you have that. But it is a trap because to have all these things, you have to pay for them. And you find that you are actually enslaved by this so-called dream. You have to get up in the morning. You have to work every day, you gotta pay for those bills. Then you realize that this house that you have, this car that you have are not a source of joy, but a source of anxiety. And tension and stress continue to build up in your life. A good many of our folks, Africans, don't go on a vacation. The vacation that I am referring to is not going back home for a visit; because when you go home to visit people expect you to give them money and solve this problem and that problem. You exhaust yourself and you come back and start all over again. Lot of times, I say to people, how many of you have taken your wife to go to the Bahamas, just go there and lie down on the beach., have a good meal, drink, and swim? We (Africans) don't do that. So the concept of American dream that means accumulation of good old things, is it really good for people? People are stressed out. I see the toll that it takes on our families, the wives and husbands. So I don't think the American dream is a magnet, it is a trap.

Ossei, from Ghana, and Madu, from Nigeria, also shared their views on the American dream by describing some of the challenges that come with achieving the American dream. Ossei explained, "When you are in America, you have a different way of looking at the American dream, but when you are outside America, you think America is like gold which everyone goes for. But it is only unfortunate that by the time you arrive in America, you start to see the realities of America, how difficult it is to make ends meet. You have to work and work your butts off in order to make ends meet." Madu simply stated, "[T]he stress, even though you are making that money or achieving the American dream, the pressure, you know, is too high. It is just too high!"

In fact, researchers have documented work-related stress on workers and their families in different cultures and populations. Consequently, it is safe to say that these immigrants were not the only ones who felt the pressure and stressors that come with achieving the American dream.

HAVE BLACK AFRICAN IMMIGRANTS ACHIEVED THE AMERICAN DREAM?

Respondents were asked if they had personally achieved their American dream. They generally paused for a few moments and reflected about their lives before giving their responses. The answers fell into three categories. Although the majority of the study participants believed in the American dream and positively defined what constituted their America dream, they mostly (62%) believed that they had not achieved it, while only 21 percent reported that they had achieved their American dream. The remaining 17% were ambiguous in their responses. They stated that, at one level, they had achieved the dream, but at another level they had not achieved it. Our study participants gave different explanations to justify their responses and described obstacles that had hindered them from either achieving or fully achieving the dream.

Respondents who had achieved their American dream

All of the 21% of respondents who reported that they had achieved their American dream mostly referred to material goods that they had accumulated and the American education that they had attained. Some also included having their family in the United States with them as their American dream. They also compared what they had accumulated in the United States to what they thought they would have had or where they would have been had they not migrated into the United States. For instance, Anita, a 45-year old registered nurse from Nigeria, explained:

> I have achieved it (American dream) because I have a family, I have a daughter, and I have a house and a car. I am working in an environment that I like. [...] I don't think I will be able to own a car if I was in Nigeria because you have to have a bulk of money to have a car so you can drive it, but here if you have a good job, then you can have a car, a home. At least they give you that opportunity to pay for it monthly. Back home, by this time, I don't think I would be able to afford a house because everything is paid for upfront. But here, you can have a 15, or a 20 to 30 year mortgage.

Just like the others, Olubami also discussed all the material goods that he had secured. However, he also compared the expectations and structure in his family relations in America to family expectations in Africa and believed that living in America had been better for him. He explained:

> All the things that I have ever done in this country, all the things that I have studied, I studied English. I taught English to the people that owned the language (means native-speakers). Feel better about that, I learned sewing and had a sewing factory in this country. I made money out of it. I have a house here. I have car back home. I have a car here. So what, I mean what do you want? I have peace here because I do not have relatives here, I do not have my in-laws, my sisters and brothers here. Here, we fight (meaning we argue), it just us (my wife and I). Then we apologize to each other and that is the end of it. But if it was in Africa, my sister would be upset that my wife told me to shut up. Of course you know the culture, the family interference in Africa.

Olubami's comments alluded to an aspect of the traditional African marriage and family that focuses on consanguineal ties. Although a man is married, in general, he still has allegiance to his family of origin (Sudarkasa 1981). It is not uncommon for the husband's family members to intervene in the functioning of the marriage and family of their male child, especially in patriarchal societies.

Respondents who had not achieved their American dream

The majority of our study participants stated that they had not achieved their American dream. Some of these respondents had some specific goals such as getting a certain degree or certification, owning a business, or obtaining a certain professional position that they had yet to reach. They also reported that they had encountered roadblocks that had slowed them down in some cases. For some, these obstacles were external factors that they could not control. Others believed that the obstacles were self- generated. Lola, a 38-year old from Nigeria, had a degree in both Business Administration and Nursing. However, her American dreams were to earn a PhD someday and also to be able to help the less fortunate. She explained:

> No, I have not yet achieved my dreams. I am still working on them and still dreaming big that I will be able to achieve my dreams and will be able to go back home or go to other less fortunate places and make a difference there. When I am able to do that, I can say I have achieved the American dream. [...] I thought I was going to go ahead and obtain a PhD, but there are certain things that came as obstacles. Like I had kids to take care of and I was working too. So those were the hindrances. But I still have that dream and one day it is going to be realized.

Richard, who wanted to be president at a community college and had achieved the human capital that would prepare him for the position, also recounted:

> No I don't think I have achieved the American dream yet. I want to become a president for a community college. I have done everything that is required. I have gotten a PhD in educational administration with a concentration in a community college leadership program. I have gone to the American Association of Community College Leadership Institute. I have attended several seminars. I have done presentations. I have published. And I am doing those things that I am supposed to do, but I have not been able to breakthrough. Okay, right now I am considering taking a job that is two steps lower than what I have so that I could move up the IT (Information Technology) side to go into the academic side of the house, hoping that would propel me back into the VP (vice president) or VC (vice chancellor) position in the academia. [...] I know those who have graduated but don't have the experience that I have had over 14 years in Community College, they don't have the experience, but the first job that they get go straight to executive level. Beside, the program that I came out of is also very competitive. The problem is that I am not the right person at the right time whenever I applied for a job. I do not want to say is a race thing, but there are people that I am more qualified than, they get higher level position jobs.

While Lola's roadblocks stemmed from some personal decisions and choices that she made, Richard's have been basically external and uncontrollable. There was a sense of frustration in his voice and the comments that he made when he talked about his experiences in the United States especially with regard to his aspirations.

Another respondent, Nana Yaa, also stated:

> I am still in the process of achieving the American dream. So that is why at 50 years of age, I'm still working on an education that will give me a chance to become a CPA (Certified Public Accountant). At that point, educationally, I would have fulfilled that part. And once I get there, I expect that will give me the opportunity for the social part, where I can get the house I want, the size I want. My children are educated to the best of their potential. At that point, they will be doing well. This is the dream for me.

When asked about the hindrances that had prevented her from achieving her dream, she explained:

> I think there have been a lot of roadblocks. That is one of the motivations for me trying to further my education. I have been working for one company for the thirteen years that I have been in this country. I notice that in this company, a lot depends on the boss. If you happen to be in the good books of the boss, regardless of who you are, how hard you work, and what education you have,

you will be promoted. […] But it doesn't seem that way in my situation. So I
have a choice to stay, leave, or better my education.

To circumvent the fact that her boss did not favorably recognize her efforts,
Nana Yaa wanted to further her education. However, this strategy may not
necessarily improve her lot because, as Richard stated earlier, he did all the
things that he thought would help, but at the end, he still did not achieve his
anticipated goal.

Kofi also explained, "Personally, I have not reached it yet. Umm, eventually, I want to have my own business. And I want people to depend on me for
a paycheck. That's my dream in life. And wherever I reside, that's what I
want to achieve and I haven't achieved that yet." When Kofi was asked about
his roadblocks, he replied, "One, I have not applied myself totally to that
dream because I have a choice. I have an alternative, I have a job, so I am not
applying myself specifically. And it seems like I am not achieving my dream
because I am not applying myself. So I can't blame anyone for that."

Whether the obstacles are external or self-generated, all the 62% of respondents who stated that they had not achieved the American dream had not
given up. They still hoped to achieve the dream someday. A point that needs
to be made here is that some of the roadblocks mentioned in this section, as
well as others, will be fully elaborated upon in the next chapters.

Respondents who had achieved the American dream to some extent, but not to their satisfaction

Participants that fell into this category generally felt that the American dream
cannot be entirely achieved because one has to continuously strive to achieve
as long as one lives. Indeed, they did not believe in putting a "ceiling" on
their lives. For them, if one agrees that one has achieved the American
dream, one must as well stop striving for better things. Also, two people in
this group expressed a fear of losing the material goods that they had acquired as long as these had not been completely paid for. For instance,
Joanna, who was living in a nice neighborhood, but still had a mortgage on
her house, did not believe that she had achieved the American dream. She
commented:

Yes I have achieved the American dream to a point. The American dream as I
read oftentimes is owning a house and making sure that you are able to take
care of your family. But, do you really own a house if you still have mortgage
to pay? It is good that you have a mortgage, but it takes time and with so many
people all over the news having their houses foreclosed, foreclosures are a
constant reminder that even though having a house is a dream, you could lose
it in a twinkling of an eye if things don't go well.

She later expounded her thoughts as follows when she was asked about the obstacles that had prevented her from achieving her dream:

> Yes, there have been a couple of roadblocks of achieving my dream—the American dream fully. I would not see it as a roadblock, but it's just a struggle within myself where even though you are here and you are settling here, your dream is to put everything that you have in the States. But at the same time, you have this conflict within you to make sure that you have something back home. I tried my best to achieve, but at the back of my mind there is this conflict within myself. Do I really want to go for all this with the mindset that one day I might leave and go back to my country of origin? So it is a conflict within myself. But America has offered me several opportunities, given me a mortgage like anybody would have wanted and a job. So I have no complaints.

Not only was Joanna, like some of the respondents, thinking about losing the American dream, but also, because they still yearned for their homelands and considered moving back, they were going through the process of "living here (America) and desiring there (homeland)." This has been an aspect of the lives of contemporary immigrants who have transnational lives.

Other respondents who have encountered some obstacles used different labels to describe the challenges. For instance, Charles, a 49-year old Nigerian immigrant, a successful self-employed man who has tried several times to run for mayor of a big city in Texas, also stated:

> No, no, no, I think the time I will use the word achieve is when I am dead. There are people who will say they have achieved the American dream, but if I say I have achieved the American dream that means I am done. I am not done yet. I have done some great things, but there are other things I still want to accomplish. [...] The American dream keeps you going all the time; even when you have it, you don't rest.

When asked about the obstacles that have slowed or deterred him from his dream, he then replied, "Of course, I have had roadblocks. However, I don't see them as roadblocks. I see them as competition. You know, you compete and then somebody wins and somebody loses. The one who fails has to find better means that will help later on."

Charles was not the only respondent who used a different label to describe challenges or roadblocks. In fact, others even refused to accept that they were being discriminated against because, for them, acknowledging this fact would not help them overcome the roadblocks. Chapter 3 discusses this issue at length.

SUMMARY

This chapter found that the American dream for black African immigrants was mainly about material possessions and the possibility to achieve material goods. Concepts such as availability of opportunities and resources were mostly evoked. Additionally, most of Crevecoeur's descriptions of what America can provide to immigrants were echoed by some respondents although Crevecoeur's writing was centuries ago. Furthermore, while some respondents thought they had achieved their American dream, other reported difficulties achieving their dream. Still others believed that they would never achieve their American dream as long as they live because a living person always has dreams. While this chapter presents some of the challenges that prevented our study participants to fully achieve their American dream, it also sets the stage for subsequent chapters.

Chapter Three

Black African Immigrants and the American Dream as Defined by James Truslow Adams

The concept of the American dream had been used prior to John Truslow Adams' famous book, The Epics of America (1931), in which he defined the American dream (Cullen 2003; Jillson 2004). However, Adams (1931) was the first person to fully provide a thorough definition for the American dream. Using his definition, African immigrants were asked: (1) Had life been better in the United States compared to life in their country of origin (had they not migrated)? (2) Had life been richer in the United States compared to life in their country of origin (had they not migrated)? (3) Had life been fuller in the United States compared to life in their country of origin (had they not migrated)? (4) Had they attained to the fullest stature of which they were innately capable? (5) Did the United States offer them opportunity according to their ability or achievement? and (6) Did people in America recognize them for what they were regardless of who they were? For each question, participants were asked to justify their answers by providing concrete explanations to substantiate their answers. Also, they were asked if they had experienced any roadblocks, and, if so, to explain the kinds of roadblocks they had experienced as well as ways they tried to overcome the obstacles.

In general, migration is a stressful and complex phenomenon where migrants leave their countries of origin, with all they have grown accustomed to, for a usually unknown life and future in a new destination. Immigrants hence experience a loss of familiarity with their homeland, language, family and friends, and their culture, as well as its values and norms (Akthar 1999; Alsop 2002; Furman 2005). The sense of loss is intensified when immigrants experience greater vicissitudes in their new country compared to the usual challenges they were used to in their old countries. In the United States, for example, these new challenges could stem from adapting to the American individualist culture and/or facing racial and ethnic issues, especially if one is a non-white immigrant and is from a culture that is more communal. All of these factors affect the adaptation process of immigrants in their host countries (Portes and Rumbaut, 2006). While the process of adapting to the new cultural and social mandates is usually strenuous and at times filled with melancholia and emptiness (Alsop 2002), once immigrants create new identities for themselves and become more knowledgeable of the culture and the social environment of the host country, they could ultimately feel strengthened and empowered (Akhar 1999; Litjmaer 2001). In some cases, immigrants become appreciative of their migratory experiences because these experiences help them create a plural identity and personality, characteristics that are practical in today's diverse world (Furman 2005). The focus of this chapter is to present the findings of the experiences of black immigrants in the context of achieving the American dream as defined by Adams.

A few points need to be made before presenting the findings. First, responses for the first three questions are presented together because they overlapped. Also, responses for the roadblocks for all six questions, along with the last question (had they thought people in America recognized them for what they were regardless of who they were?), were presented together for the same reason. Second, some of the participants (10%) had issue with the questions that asked them to compare their lives in the United States to their lives back home had they not migrated. They thought these questions were difficult to answer because they left their native countries very young and had been in the United States for a long time. While we agreed that the questions were somewhat difficult, they at least allowed respondents to analyze their lived American experiences and compare them to whatever experiences they had in their native countries prior to migrating, as well as their experiences whenever they go back home to visit. Third, all of the respondents (especially the ones who immigrated when they were children) had had a chance to return to their countries of origin for a visit since immigrating. Hence, they were able to recover their abandoned childhood (Behar 1996) and/or somewhat heal the pain of fragmentation that they might have endured having left these countries so young (Ibieta 2001). Thus, this healing experience helped them answer the questions in a non-emotional way. In the end, all of the study participants provided answers to all of the questions, by at times comparing their lives in the United States to those of their relatives, friends, and classmates they had left behind.

While most of the respondents reported that their lives in America had been better, richer, and fuller compared to what they thought their lives would have been in their home countries had they not migrated, they specifically recounted some ways in which their lives had been worse off or unfulfilling in the United States. Specifically, they described obstacles they encountered living in the United States as immigrants and black.

HAD LIFE BEEN BETTER, RICHER, AND FULLER IN THE UNITED STATES?

Overall, responses provided by study participants for these questions (had life been better, richer, and fuller in the United States compared to what their life would have been in their country of origin had they not migrated?) fell into three themes: social structure in America, betterment of oneself in America, and an incomplete life in America. Each major theme is described in the following sections.

Social structure in the United States

In this study, social structure is defined as the characteristics and organizations of American society. Black African immigrants in the United States come in contact with these characteristics and organizations daily. Consequently, they were influenced by them and reacted to them. Also it is important to note that these characteristics and organizations became some of the agents of their socialization in their new sociocultural environment. Further, to use Bourdieu's idea (1977), the American social structure thus becomes part of their habitus. In fact, as immigrants in our study learned ways to evaluate and cope with new and unpredicted challenges that came their way in the United States, the American norms, values, beliefs, and expectations that were part of their everyday social lives also cognitively influenced the norms, values, beliefs, and expectations that they held prior to immigrating. Additionally, as they interacted with Americans, their experiences, beliefs, and behaviors changed accordingly. Nonetheless, as immigrants from different social environments, the cultural backgrounds they had acquired in their home countries impacted their views, analyses, and interpretations of their interactions and their daily lived experiences in America. Therefore, these immigrants developed a system of dispositions (habitus) that helped them deal with issues that immigrant groups generally face regardless of their ascribed status such as country of origin and/or race. But, as black immigrants in America, they also faced and dealt with "situations most frequent for the members" of their racial group (Bourdieu 1977, 85).

Almost all of the respondents (90%) believed that the social structure in America had allowed them to improve themselves and their lives compared to what their lives would have been in their home countries. The structures of the different social institutions such as the political system (democracy and freedom), the educational system, the socioeconomic system, security and law enforcement, and others were mentioned as reasons for the betterment of their lives. Also, they compared how things were done culturally, economically, politically, and socially in America to their countries of origin. Moreover, some believed that poverty and corruption in Africa had not permitted ordinary Africans to make progress. Others reported that some African cultural practices, such as one's obligation to extended kinship, restricted one's ability to fully develop and/or use her/his potential.

In the following comments, Madu talked about the resources that America provides to make life easier for its people:

> My life here is better in the sense that it's not a struggle to live here. In Nigeria, it's a struggle to get from point A to point B because of bad roads. You have to contend with no electricity. Those aspects of life, there is no question, it's a whole lot better here. And the security aspect also is better. You are not worried that somebody is going to break into your house while you are sleeping. Even though this may happen here, it's more of a worry in Nigeria for instance than here. From that point of view, it's better here.

As commented above, problems with transport infrastructure are widespread in Africa. Rural transport conditions are substantially poor (Platteau 1996; Porter 2002), making travel very challenging and at times even precarious. Additionally, criminality has been on the rise in urban areas in Africa as a whole. However, African countries do not have the necessary infrastructure to combat the crimes. Hence, as reported by Cilliers, Hughes, and Moyer (2011), criminalized violence will be one of the significant challenges for African authorities in the near future. Thus, as reported in the previous chapter, security was an important factor that our participants thought about when they compared life in the United States to life in their home countries.

Akim, a 64-year-old professor at a community college, explained how America provided resources and helped people to be efficient and productive. He also compared some of the American cultural practices to the African ways of doing things:

> Life is better here because I wake up every morning and I feel that everything is in place for me to get things accomplished. The resources are there, and I do get those things that I love accomplished. In Nigeria on the other hand, the system is structured in such a way that no matter what you do, it is difficult to have things done in a timely manner. Sometimes, corruption and bribery are expected. This is so because of the structure of the system which does not allow for quick results.

Akim later discussed how the extended family may at times make life difficult for one in general:

The extended family, I am not saying that this isn't good, it's good, but the extended family has a lot of folks looking up to you to help them out. If you don't, it's another crisis. Food that is for three, twenty people would like to feed on that. Again, they have to share. That's how we've been brought up. America is a little bit individualistic. That is their culture. That's the way they have been brought up. I'm not blaming anybody for that. We Africans too should be able to figure it out quickly. And those of us who are educated are supposed to maybe help shape up the structure that we love to see in Africa. Again, life here is better because you're open minded. You can do what you want to do, you can say what you want to say. That is probably because of the quality of democracy in this country.

Like some of his fellow African immigrants in this study, Kuma also explained why life in America was fuller to him by focusing on all the family problems and expectations that he would have been entangled with in his home country had he not migrated to the United States:

Yeah, I think life in America is fuller. Back in Ghana, there are too many family problems there. See, like in my family, I'm the oldest brother, son. So, all the problems in the family will be on you. So, one cannot move up. Where you go, the problems will drag you down. [...] money, leadership, anything that is hard thing, they bring it to you to solve. If you are the oldest person in your family, no matter what problem someone got, they bring it to you and expect you to solve it. Although you are not the one who created the problem, they come to you to find a solution to that problem.

In some of the African cultures, the oldest son is considered the "chief" of the family or "family head" and hence oversees the well-being of the family as a whole. He is the one that resolves issues that befall the family members. At times, these duties can be overwhelming for one person to tackle. Also, the nature of the problem will warrant whether or not one goes beyond the immediate family for advice.

Also, Kwaku, who had earned a bachelor's degree in Systems Analysis and Business Administration, explained how the American social and economic system allows one to achieve an upward mobility regardless of her/his fortuitous and un-fortuitous traits.

Yes, on average, I think my life has been better. I have achieved a higher degree in America and also relative to the average Ghanaian and my classmates. There is one thing that jumped at me when I read the definition. That is social order. I think this is embedded in the American society in the sense that there are steps that one needs to take to get to a certain place in this society. Not because you know somebody or because you are born into this family or that family.

Just like Kwaku, most of the participants admired the American meritocratic system because they believed that people were judged based on their talent and skills instead of their family backgrounds and networks. It is important to note that most Americans also espouse this belief of the United States being a meritocratic nation (McNamee and Miller, 2004), which is what makes the American dream appealing to most Americans because they believe that hard work is justly rewarded.

Another aspect of life in America that respondents appreciated was equality and equity between the sexes. Abeba's comments embodied those of the respondents who admired the ways females and males are treated in America, although she acknowledged that America still has a way to go with regard to equity between the sexes. She recounted:

> Yeah, life in America is better. I visited Ethiopia some time ago and my husband and I talked about it. There, we noticed there is a difference between men and women. We knew there is wage differences and all that. But here, it is not open. I could never live there. People really treat women differently there. They have no respect for women. If you are not with a man, it is hard to get service. Here, I think men and women are almost treated the same, until you go deep and dig. Then you will find some differences.

While the United States as well as other Western countries have been on the battlefield for gender and women's rights for nearly a century (O'Connor, Orloff, and Shaver, 1999), women in low-income countries with strong patriarchal norms are still struggling for their basic rights. This becomes obvious when one visits any of such countries.

Overall, the social structure in the United States certainly impacted the views of participants. After living in America, they were able to come up with a list of all that they thought was wrong in their place of origin compared to the United States. Also, their mindsets, outlooks, and expectations in life had definitely changed because of what they had lived and/or experienced in the United States. They had acquired a new habitus that guided their norms and values.

Betterment of oneself in the United States

Respondents believed that American society had taught them how to be self-reliant and hardworking. It had also given them a can-do spirit. Furthermore, they believed they had been exposed to different ideologies that had led them to have an open mind. Also they had acquired new skills in doing different activities that were important life skills helping them to be successful. Consequently, some even reported that they had imparted these new skills to friends and family back home whenever they had a chance. For example, Mouna, from Ghana, explained:

Being here in America, I have been exposed to different ideas. I have become a spokesperson to a lot of my friends back home. In America, one has to be hardworking and diligent at work. In Africa, everyone has a maid. But here, you have to do everything on your own. This disciplines you in every area. So that has helped me a lot in my personal life as well as my professional life.

Fausty, a 45-year old woman with an associate degree in Computer Science, also described how being in the United States had helped her acquire some life skills because of the ways American society is structured:

Hmmm, well, I would say I am richer compared to my friends in Ghana. What I got, they don't have. I got advancement, but they don't have advancement. I think I've been wiser, smart, and responsible. You know how Africa is. You sit over there and you go, 'hey Mary pick up the stuff. Mary clean up the dishes, Mary, wash my clothes.' Here there is no Mary. So that keeps you active or motivated all the time, you know. You don't have to rely on anybody. You do it yourself. But that's one good thing about it. It keeps you strong and keeps you going. It makes you advance.

In Africa, because of poverty, labor is inexpensive and almost anyone can afford a maid, especially in urban settings. At times, these maids are very young, especially if they are from rural areas as oftentimes parents in rural areas entrust their children to relatives and others in urban settings to be raised. Hence, it costs practically nothing to have these young maids. They also tend to do most of the tedious household chores (Blunt 2001). Contrary to the United States where labor is costly, it is impossible for the average American to have a maid. Thus, some Africans find life difficult when they first immigrate to a Western society because they no longer had help, as indicated in chapter one and in the comments above. However, learning to do all the chores by oneself became a strength according some of the respondents, as one became self-reliant.

For other respondents, it was their accumulated knowledge and skills that made them better people. Charles explained how his accumulated experiences in the United States had given him an edge over his fellow Ghanaians:

I would say yes, my life has been richer because of all the experiences I've had here. Not just education, but practical experiences in a lot of ways. I have colleagues, you know, that after high school stayed in Ghana, went to the local universities, and stayed in the Ghanaian system. And when I go back and visit, sometimes I can see that the experiences that I got here, not only in the United States, because I had a job that took me all around the world, had prepared me to be more practical. So I got much richer experiences overall. It is because I happened to be in a position here in the United States that gave me more than my colleagues back home in Ghana.

Even though most of the respondents showed appreciation for all that the United States had offered and allowed them to achieve, they nonetheless reported significant problems they had to endure as immigrants and black. The following section examines these issues.

Incomplete life in the United States

While respondents mostly agreed that life in the United States had been better and somewhat richer for them, they also stated that their social lives had been, at best, incomplete. For some, issues such as a lack of a social life, missing their family, holidays, and the pressure of work were some of the factors that prevented their lives in the United States from being full. For others, racial injustices were major factors that made their lives unfulfilled.

Joanna, a 35-year old Ghanaian who had been in the US since 1999, explained why her life in America had not been fuller:

> No, my life in America, I don't think has been fuller because I miss my family.
> The family, you know, can give you all the support. I miss my mom, my other
> siblings and my children also miss their cousins. I even realized this more
> when we vacationed in Ghana not long ago. When it comes to money, my life
> is full here, but I'm missing a lot.

When asked about things that she did to overcome the void of not having her family with her, she stated:

> I have a large phone bill every month because I call my parents twice a week
> to speak to them and then maybe once a week to speak to my siblings. This is
> just to compensate for the fact that I don't get to see them often. So that is one
> of the things that I deal with, and then I watch African movies and try to speak
> my language of origin to my children so that I can impact something of my
> origin on them.

Indeed, Joanna used different methods in order to feel close to loved ones and her country of origin. As explained by Akthar (1995), to bridge the gap between their home country and their host country, immigrants use some modalities such as calling their home country, listening to music in their native language, and/or speaking their native language.

Darwit from Ethiopia also explained his experiences of not having a complete life in the United States:

> I have a fuller life in some ways. But if you really think about the social life,
> no! All we do here is watch T.V. We don't do that there. There are always
> people you sit around and talk to. You talk to your grandparents there. Here, I
> miss that aspect of social life. As far as the other aspect of life, such as

financial opportunities, we have them here. And life is better here in that sense. But socially, no, you miss your culture. The holidays are not the same.

In general, immigrants go through some complex and ambiguous life experiences where the culture of the host country is compared to that of the home country, especially during important events such as holidays. During these times, immigrants may feel intense loss of the familiar and routine activities that are part of their lives prior to migrating. Not feeling being fully a part of the host society can become intense and painful (Alsop 2002). Also, at times, this may lead to what Akthar (1999, 123) called "retrospective idealization," whereby immigrants look at their experiences in their old world and whatever symbolizes their home country positively and with joy.

Jethro, a 50-year old man who went to Nigeria, his home country, after a short visit and returned to America about five months before the interview explained:

> Well, richer in the sense of financially, I would say yes. But for one reason, each time I go home, I don't know what it is, each time I go home, it does not matter what I am eating, it does not matter how bad the situation is, I feel at rest. I feel like I am, you know, I don't have any worry. I feel so fulfilled. I can sit down and not think about anything. And I came back here with all this, what we call riches here, and it is not the same. I never can figure it out what it is. I don't know if you feel the same way when you go home or if you don't, I mean.

This feeling of "missing something" has been discussed in immigration discourse. For instance, van Ecke (2005), talking about the feeling of loss that immigrants go through, stated: "No matter how great life in the new country is, at times we all miss the feelings of being surrounded with the people, sounds, smells and insights that constitute back home" (468). While Jethro may not be able to identify what is missing in his life in the United States, he feels complete whenever he returns to his home country, a feeling that some of his fellow respondents mentioned quite often.

Another common theme that was used to explain why life in America was not a full life for our study participants was racial injustice. Osaze did not mince his words when he discussed the general status of blacks in the United States as well as in other societies:

> No, life is not fuller in America. I talk to my people here a lot. I say to them: 'you and I are struggling here to raise our children up to become in fact black Americans, the same way we become black Germans, black Koreans. That puts you in the lower stratum of society, the bottom, you know. So we are struggling to get our kids to be accepted at the bottom of the society. That's really what it means, whether you like it or not. Well, that's the way things are. Why is it like that in Germany? Why is it like that in the U.K? Why is it like

that in Sweden or Korea? The only place where it is not like that is in Africa. And we are leaving Africa to come to places where we and our kids are second class citizens.

Richard's comments below also exemplified some of the feelings of not being accepted that respondents expressed:

No, we don't have a fuller life, because you still have the issue of this society, hmm, not belonging because you are a foreigner. No matter how many years you live in America, no matter what you have done [accomplished], you still feel that way. You are not fully accepted. You are still an outsider, and I think we overcompensate for that. Okay, there are so many Nigerians walking around with terminal degrees, with PhDs, D.Ed degrees, and so on. I venture to bet that if it were white peoples, they would have stopped somewhere after they had acquired a certain degree. They would have stopped because they would have been making enough progress and would have had satisfaction that comes with having degrees. This is not the case with us Africans. So we keep trying to get that satisfaction. We say to ourselves, 'well if I can't achieve this status with my education, let me get more education and maybe that would get me to where I want to be. That is what I think! Personally, if I had gotten the job that I wanted and was making the money that I wanted, probably, I would not have gotten a PhD even though I have always wanted a PhD.

The comments above reflect the sentiments of most respondents vis à vis race relations in America. However, this theme will be fully examined when responses for the roadblocks and for the sixth question (did people in America recognize participants for what they were regardless of who they were) are presented later in the chapter.

Before presenting the rest of the findings, note that two of the participants stated that their lives would have been similar to their lives in the United States had they not migrated. Two also mentioned that they were doing as well or even better in their countries of origin before migrating. One reported that because of her family background and connections, she would have had similar a life back home. Another participant thought that the drive in him that had made his life a success in America would have made him successful back home as well. Fred, a 61-year old, who migrated from Ghana in 1972, explained:

I think I'd have made a life in Ghana as here. Frankly speaking, in terms of who I am, the drive I have in me, if you take me and put me in any environment I will do well. Whether I live in a poor country or not, I think I will make a life for myself. So I don't think I can say my life would have been any better or worse had I not migrated. I think I make conscientious choices very early that I was going to study, work, and live here. So either way, if I was in Ghana right now, I would probably be the same as what I am doing right now, or even more so. I wouldn't say that by living here I am better off.

Furthermore, three of the respondents stated that their lives in America were not better, richer, or fuller. They all had personal difficulties in addition to some racial challenges. Carlos' experiences embodied the lives of the other two. He shared his experiences and disappointment:

> No, my life is not better, richer, or fuller at all. The career path I have taken, the career I chose was such that I had many obstacles to overcome. When I first started over 20 years ago, even though the company encouraged me to abandon my MBA and work for them and then once I got started with them, they will have me finish my MBA, they never followed through. It annoyed me back then, when I found out that they were hiring me as somebody to fulfill their Equal Opportunity requirements because they saw another black brilliant person.
>
> Later on, I had to overcome quite a few discriminatory practices with my initial employer, like telling me I couldn't talk to valued clients who are white. I could not talk to them, but bring them to my white colleagues or have my white colleagues talk to them. I should talk to the blacks, for example. You know, discrimination was very overt back then to a point I ended up suing that employer in a federal court for discrimination. The thing is when they realized that I had white clients, they tried to sabotage me. So, I left that employer years ago, it was in 1993.
>
> Overall, no! In my effort to make a better life I have abandoned the dreams that I had. I had for example a dream of becoming a lawyer since growing up. In fact, in 1992-1993, I gained admission to the University of Kansas to go to the law school. But, the requirement was that I had to quit working for a full year, you know, to concentrate that first year in law school without distraction. So my educational dream was about to be fulfilled. My dad's aspiration for me was to have a Ph.D one day. But I abandoned all of that because I had to make money to take care of myself, take care of family, pay school fees for siblings at home and other extended family. So in a sense, no! If I were in Nigeria, if I had gone to school in Nigeria, probably I would have accomplished all my educational aspirations. And so that is, there is a disparity between the way America functions, the concept of America dream is sold to us, how we the people from Africa understand it and the reality on the ground. I spent 25 years of my life in financial services, business; yes, I have fortunately achieved the qualifications and now companies recognize me bringing them business. But, that's like a little fish in a big ocean. If I had chosen any field in Africa, in Nigeria particularly and put the amount of energy and time I have devoted to my career, I would have bagged a little more than I have here.

While Carlos' experiences were not similar to that of most of respondents in our study, especially with regard to experiencing overt discrimination and taking a legal action against one's employer, these are nonetheless common among African Americans, especially older African Americans. As documented in her book, The Black Elite, Benjamin (2005) explained the experiences of black professionals in order to show that this elite group does not necessarily transcend the racial barrier just because of their achieved status.

HAD THEY ATTAINED TO THE FULLEST STATURE OF WHICH THEY WERE INNATELY CAPABLE?

Responses to the fourth question "had participants attained to the fullest stature of which they were innately capable" are presented here. Only 12% reported that they had attained to the fullest stature of which they were innately capable. These respondents stated that they had accomplished things that they had set out to do, such as getting a higher education, having a good-paying job, and having their family join them. However, 77% of respondents felt that they were innately capable of attaining more than what they had attained. Various reasons were given for their lack of reaching their full potential: not knowing the American system and not having mentors to consult for counsel, putting limits on oneself as to what one could do, not being too committed to one's goals, and family responsibilities in the United States as well as in their countries of origin. Also, some respondents simply felt that one could not possibly achieve to the fullest stature of which one is innately capable as long as one still lives. For these respondents, one has to continuously aspire to reach new heights.

Maria's comments exemplified some of the respondents' reasons for not achieving their full potential. She was 48 years old and migrated from Kenya in 1978. She had a Master's degree in Nursing, but she wanted to eventually earn a doctoral degree. She commented:

> You have limited resources to go around. You have to pay for your student loan, mortgage, and all the other bills. That's a struggle. Then, you have to take care of your family here. You want to make sure that the children are getting the right education. And then you are getting older and you wonder if you can again start going to school. At the same time, you are trying to help somebody in Africa. Okay, then you have a nephew here, he needs your help financially. All of these responsibilities kind of tire you out.

A lot of immigrants have an obligation, especially a financial one, toward family and relatives they left behind as well as to those who are in the United States. Evidence suggests that the growth of immigrant population correlates with the growth of remittances that are sent back each year to relatives that are left behind (Giuliano and Ruiz-Arranz, 2005).

Yemisi was among those who believed that their own lack of effort or motivation was to blame. She explained her situation as follows:

> No, I don't think I have achieved my goal which I had initially set for myself. I think many of the setbacks have been my own thing, you know, because I didn't push myself as hard, you know. My recent goal was to go back to school, finish my schooling and get my degree in physical therapy. That's what I have eventually planned for. Um, but I got married and got little bit

distracted. Um, I can't use that much as an excuse because my sister did the same thing and got married, you know, got a baby, but she continued her education and she finished it. We had the same plan, but with me, I guess, it's mainly like your own personality; how you push yourself, what's really important for you. And I just, um, education is very important for me, but I guess, I didn't push myself. I gave myself an excuse. You know, that's what it is. I gave myself an excuse that I am too tired, just can't do it right now.

Carlos was one of the respondents who wished they had a mentor who advised them about how things work in their profession as well as in other areas. He recounted:

> I have not attained to the fullest of what I am innately capable because I lost precious time trying to overcome individual and professional obstacles that I wasn't prepared for. Because I had nobody to give me directions, I had no mentors. Professionally, I had no mentors. I had to learn a lot of things by trial and error and that is not the way to achieve success. You don't achieve success by trial and error. You achieve success if you have a pattern you can follow. There is nobody that can guide you in case they see that you are making an error. Hmm, they can redirect you. But unfortunately for me, if I am on a path which is the wrong path, because I don't have that corrective mechanism where somebody can just advise me, by the time I realize it, I am too far gone. And by the time I backtrack and decide to go this way or that way, I have lost several months, I have lost a year.

Lacking mentors is not unique to just black Africans but people in minority groups in general. Indeed, the importance of mentoring in professional as well as non-professional organizations has been documented (Thomas 2001; Adams 1997; Heinen and O'Neil, 2004). In general, because of a lack of mentors, minority members' career progression is not up to par with their white counterparts (Thomas 2001). Through mentoring, new workers learn the "ropes" and politics of an institution. Additionally, workers who have mentors tend to be more successful than their counterparts who do not have mentors (Blancero and Del Campo, 2005; Thomas 2001). Thus, as Carlos described his situation, many minorities are affected by not having mentors to guide them in their jobs, a situation that makes them lag behind their white counterparts.

Nine people believed that one could never attain to the fullest stature of which one is innately capable because as one lives, one has to aspire to reach new heights. Richard's comments below exemplified this sentiment. He explained:

> No, but thank God! No, because you have to keep giving yourself opportunity for growth. If you have attained all that is to attain, you might as well die. We have to still keep aspiring, keep trying to improve no matter what. That's why I do all these things, that's why I keep doing professional development stuff,

still trying to publish, still trying to write and present at conferences whenever
I can , getting involved in, hmm, in community activities and developing
leadership qualities and stuff.

DOES THE UNITED STATES OFFER OPPORTUNITY ACCORDING TO ABILITY OR ACHIEVEMENT?

Seventy one percent of respondents believed that America offered opportunity according to ability or achievement, while 21% reported that this did not
happen all the time, and 8% believed that America did not offer opportunity
according to ability or achievement. Almost all of the respondents who
thought the United States had a fair system whereby opportunities were
available to those with ability and achievement used two important concepts
embedded in the American culture to justify their positions: 1. with hard
work one can achieve anything and 2. meritocracy.

Some believed that they just needed to work hard in order to achieve
whatever they wanted. For example, Abeba explained her point, "Oh definitely, America does offer opportunity according to ability or achievement. I
really do believe that I could be what I want to be. I really think I can be the
person who I really want to be. I just have to make some sacrifices and work
hard."

Others, although they thought there might be some challenges that may
hamper them in achieving their goals, still believed that, with determination,
these obstacles could be overcome. Keith elaborated:

> Yes, absolutely, because there is no roadblock that you cannot overcome. It is
> easier to blame somebody else if you do not achieve something than actually
> overcoming that challenge. There are doctors, pilots who are Africans and
> doing amazingly well in this country. We have a black president. You need to
> have a strong state of mind to become successful in this country. Yes, there
> could be some racism but we have that in Kenya as well. There is racism
> against Somalis. They don't get as many opportunites as the Kenyans. But
> then there are some Somalis who are doing better than Kenyans. I learned that
> before I came to the United States not to use an excuse and it has worked
> wonders for me.

Fausty simply put it as follows, "Yes, because they have a system here where
education is not about race, it's not about age, you know. Even if you are
about 100 years old, but have the needed credentials and are capable of doing
the job, they will give it to you. So that gives you the ability to achieve your
goals."

While the majority of the respondents found America fair because it
offered opportunity according to ability and/or achievement, others questioned the validity of this belief. In fact 29% of our study participants either

had some reservations toward the American meritocratic system or thought that America actually did not offer opportunity according to ability or achievement. For instance, Anthony, a retired Ghanaian who had worked in corporate America, was one of the few respondents who had an ambivalent position about the American meritocratic system. Although he believed that hard work pays off, he also explained that one had to give everything that one had in order to make it in America. He explained:

> Yes and no! Yes, in the sense that you have to work hard and prove yourself above and beyond what is expected. And no, in the sense that nobody wants to bring you along if you are not pulling up your bootstraps, you know, if you are not doing anything. So America will not offer you anything, they will make you get by if you are mediocre. [...] Unless you are born into wealth, you cannot make it by getting by. So that is where the yes and no come from.

Bandele's experiences typified the lives of those who did not believe that the United States offered opportunity according to ability and achievement. He was a 60-year old professor who had been in the United States for over 30 years. He recounted his experiences:

> No, you have to actually look at the concept of the American dream. You are supposed to go for it and look for it, and kind of achieve it. Now, the problem is that in the process of trying to look for it, there are roadblocks: discrimination, racism, credit issues. These are what I consider inherent roadblocks. I have applied for positions for which I think I am much more capable for than those who were actually hired. You apply for positions you know you are good for, but yet you don't get the position. So, it's so discouraging. At this moment, at this point, I am an adjunct lecturer at the University and I have been doing that since 1987. That's like what? Over twenty years now! There have been full time positions, tenure track positions in my area of expertise. Even though I am much more qualified, yet those jobs are not given to me when I applied. There have been many that have been hired since I have been at this university.

When asked how he would explain the fact that he had been working for the same department as an adjunct for years, but had not been able to get a full time, tenure track position, he proceeded:

> There is no justification for my situation. That is where the subtle discrimination might be perceived when you know you are very qualified and experienced and your work also shows it, yet you still don't get a position that you deserve.

Although only a minority of our study participants either had ambivalent views of or did not believe in the American meritocratic system, some scholars and writers have questioned the validity of a meritocracy, a core value of the American dream, by denouncing not only the fact that, originally, America was not created equally for all people, but also how the prospects of achieving the America dream are dwindling in present-day America. Jillson (2004) discussed ways that minority populations, blacks, and women, for example, were excluded from achieving the American dream. These people were exploited and subjugated for a very long time. However, they fought and still continue to fight for a chance to rise economically or socially. Also, McClelland and Tobin (2010) are among Americans who believe that the chances for ordinary Americans to achieve the American dream are dwindling since the system is becoming less and less meritocratic. Additionally, Solis (2005) wrote about the experiences of the few black executives who had achieve success and some of the biases that they had to overcome to prove that America is not as meritocratic as most tend to believe.

WERE RESPONDENTS RECOGNIZED FOR WHAT THEY WERE REGARDLESS OF WHO THEY WERE?

The idea that the United States has become a level playing field where anyone regardless of her/his ascribed status, especially race, can achieve social mobility through sheer determination and effort has become a normative belief in contemporary America, especially among whites. Also, public opinion polls and researchers show that race relations in the United States are constantly improving with time (Greeley and Sheatsley, 1971; Firebaugh and Davis, 1988; Taylor, Sheatsley, and Greeley, 1978). Although it is true that race relations have improved, and racism has declined relative to what it used to be from the time of Jim Crow laws in the South that led to de jure discrimination, to the de facto discrimination that was prevalent in the North, scholars and activists would be quick to remind us that it is only the overt type of racism that has disappeared and it has been replaced by what is called modern racism (McConahay 1986) or new racism (Bonilla-Silva 2010). Several studies have indicated that Americans no longer show openly racist ideologies and acts since racism has become legally and socially unacceptable. Hence, to be politically correct, racism is expressed in ways that are more subtle and difficult to detect (Dovidio and Gaertner, 1996; McConahay, Hardee, and Batts, 1981; Bonilla-Silva 1997; Bonilla-Silva 2010). In fact, a new racial rhetoric has been adopted whereby racist views and ideologies are indirectly expressed.

In this era of modern racism, different means are used, especially by some whites in America as elsewhere, to justify racially divisive acts and ideas such as nationalism and national identity. Although nationalism has different implications, as argued by Mavroudi (2010), its core notions are based on the desire for purity and homogeneity, concepts that are exclusionary. Immigration is then considered a threat for nationalism since immigrants breed diversity. Additionally, in the name of nationalism, some whites believe that they are the proprietors of a nation's valued and scarce resources and thus have to protect these from others who are construed as different. The differences could be cultural, political, social, etc. From this standpoint, people play on the differences between themselves and the other group(s), usually demonizing the other. This systematically leads to conflictual inter-group relations. Furthermore, because the volume of global migration has significantly increased in the past few decades (United Nations 2002), immigration and its related issues have created divisions in the United States as well as in other Western societies (Esses, Jackson, and Armstrong, 1998).

Another characteristic of modern racism is color-blindness (Bonilla-Silva and Forman, 2000; Bonilla-Silva 2002; Gallagher 2003). Color-blindness comes into play when some of the old, stereotypical ideologies such as cultural differences among different racial groups are used to justify racial inequality. Additionally, since it has become socially unacceptable to express one's racist thoughts, some whites carefully choose certain words to explain their ideologies on racial issues without portraying themselves as racists. The fact is that they do not want to appear as racist, thus, expressing slippery and ambivalent views regarding racial issues (Bonilla-Silva 2002). Because of these beliefs and practices, non-whites in the United States as well as in other western societies still suffer unfair treatment and injustices (Bonilla-Silva 2000).

With regard to our study participants, several of them were not recognized for what they were, but who they were (black and immigrant) was taken into consideration instead. This created different kinds of roadblocks in their processes of achieving the American dream. Some reported that they were not appreciated in their work place. Others reported that they were not justly rewarded for their work. Some even stated that they were labeled as people who were taking jobs away from native-born Americans. Still others were not given the same opportunities as their white counterparts. However, despite these difficulties, most of the respondents devised some strategies that, in the end, helped them achieve a better life.

Anita's experiences typified some of the challenges that participants had to go through in the work place. In her first job, some of her coworkers viewed her as someone who was stealing jobs from Americans. She stated, "There was a day when they fired one of my coworkers because of me. This person told me that I should go back to my country because we came to steal their jobs." Anita explained that this person was fired that day because she and some friends had problems previously with some other African workers. Thus, this was the second time that this particular worker had issues with a non-American born coworker. As stated earlier, this individual may be considered a nationalist who believed that she had to protect the interests of her fellow American-born workers from foreign-born people.

Additionally, when Anita started to work in a big hospital in the Dallas area, her accent was a significant struggle that she had to overcome. She explained:

> There are a lot of roadblocks that I had to overcome. When I began my first job, nobody really wanted to work with me and nobody would understand a word of what I was saying. They said that maybe I was speaking my native language. I then had to look for foreign nurses and befriend and work with them. However, later on when they realized my value (I help anyone in need), they respected me and I respected them.

She also recounted some of the experiences she had with her employer and some of her coworkers with regard to her wages:

> When I was working in 'Big Hospital,' I took the job as an RN (Registered Nurse). I did not know what I was qualified for. Thus, I was offered $25 per hour for part-time and I quickly accepted it. So, it was one day, when I was doing my evaluation, people (co-workers) told me the money they were getting. They were making $27 per hour. I then told the lady that was evaluating us that I don't know what I did to the director because I am making $25 per hour while others are making $27 per hour. So she said she will talk to the director. It was not long after that, about 3 months, after that they gave me a full time job and rectified the pay too.

When Anita was asked how she coped with all the challenges, she explained:

> I am a person that believes in God. God is always there for you regardless of the situation. So I always have religion in the back of my mind, especially in a situation where you have people who are like, "I don't know what you are speaking." I always told them, 'you calm down and listen. I studied English in school. You just have to be calm and listen.' I really like people who have traveled around the world. They are softer and listen to you carefully because they have seen and met different kinds of people.

Others also encountered different forms of prejudice, stereotypes, and discrimination. Anthony, a 61-year old Ghanaian who retired from corporate America and had his own business, described some of the obstacles he experienced:

> When you deal with a lot of bigots in this country, you will realize that their thinking is different; because they think black Americans are mediocre performers. They cannot put aside that belief and give you the opportunity to do your work. There have been occasions where I have set up some business deals over the phone, you know. Then, the people would want to meet you in person.

Sometimes, I decided to meet the folks in person and they were shocked to find out that I was black. And after that I could see that because they were bigots, they did not want to continue the business deals. The deals eventually died. [...] that was one example to show you that people would not work with you because you are black. It is all bigotry, and that is the way I look at it. It was their loss, not mine, even though we did not do business. And I would not do any business with a bigot, you know. I will not feel comfortable working with them anyway. There are other people out there that I can work with.

When Anthony was asked about how he overcomes these roadblocks, he explained:

Avoidance is one of the ways. And again, it is my nature that if somebody truly feels that they are superior to me as a human being and not because of my abilities, I don't have any business, you know, dealing with them. [...] another way is perseverance. Regardless of the race issue, if you are a good person and you do a good job, even though there are bigots still around who will not appreciate you for the color of your skin, I think that if you just do a good job, you will succeed.

Another respondent, Osaze, a retired surgeon who had practiced in both Canada and the United States, shared how he felt unappreciated at work in America and described ways that he tried to make his professional life meaningful:

You understand that I worked in Canada before migrating to America. I lived there for 6 years. I lived in a small community. There, people were really appreciative a whole lot and I had tremendous satisfaction as a surgeon working there, even though I never made as much money as I made here in the United States. But here, particularly in a place like Houston, there was tremendous competition. And some people don't even want you to be there. [...] and they are looking for ways to get you out. So, I mean, how can you really feel in good conscience that you are contributing? For your own sanity, you feel like you are contributing and you devise ways to contribute. So, I made it a policy when I was practicing that any kids, any Africans, particularly those who were driving cabs and wanted medical exams, I would give them the exams free of charge. So, from that point of view, I contributed in my own circle and was appreciated, I must say, but the society at large, I don't know. [...] the struggle of life as a foreign black doctor was quite challenging. Anyway, everywhere I go, I always find that I am the first person and I am laying the trail for others. I was the first to get in to (Grand Hospital) in Houston. As the first black doctor, I had to fight to get in and stay in.

Steven, a successful business owner who originally came from Nigeria, talked about some of his challenges and his philosophy about life in general, especially the challenges that he faced when he tried to run for mayor in one of the biggest cities in Texas:

You know, there is the issue of ethnicity and racism. These will always be with us. I had some issues when I was trying to run for mayor in (big city). They tried to kick me out of the ballot, but I prevailed. My name was withdrawn because someone said that 'we don't want an African to become our mayor.' Some council members protested, but my name was withdrawn. I took my case to court and I won, since I am an American citizen just like the other candidates for the mayoral race. [...] I will say that some particular individual(s) did not want me to be on the ballots, you know, to be fair, it is not America that did not, but some individual(s). For other Americans, I would be a perfect candidate. As a matter of fact, in 1987, I was the first foreign-born American to be elected the secretary of the Black Chamber of Commerce in (big city). Then I became a member of the city council. I do not let what people think about me stop me, my dreams. I will always apply for whatever I need and if I see injustice, I will use my right to fight for it, you know. [...]. You know, sometimes I don't see these things as roadblocks, I see them as competition. When you compete, someone wins and someone loses. You know, you want to be with your homeboys, you prefer them because you can relate to them easily. We do that back home too. We will give the contracts, first, to Nigerians if there are people from Togo around.

Finally, a few participants had difficulties interpreting some of the odd be-haviors and treatments that they received from their superiors and bosses. As shown in the comments below by Mrs. Djoa who had difficulty understand-ing the insidious nature of the unfair treatment that she received at work:

Yes, you have to work harder than everybody else to prove yourself. And also, there's some form of tacit discrimination because you might be doing, you know, as well as your colleagues, but the recognition goes with them. And you can't really put your finger on why someone makes the progress whilst you are not making the progress. If you go, judging from the average, you are doing equally good or even better. That's a gray area, you can't really put your finger on it, but if you open your eyes, you know, it's some form of discrimination. We're not used to it. So that's another hindering factor.

All the comments above showed that black Africans face issues of prejudice, stereotyping, and discrimination. However, there were different strategies that participants used in order to overcome racial and place of origin-related biases. For instance, some of them did not want to use these challenges as excuses to fail in their endeavors and refused to accept either their existence or downplayed them as in the case of Keith who believed that one can always overcome the effects of discrimination. He used the example of Kenya, his homeland where Somalis are discriminated against, but some find ways to strive regardless of the discriminatory behaviors that Kenyans exhibit toward them. Others acknowledged the challenges but trusted their faith to see them through. Still! others, such as Anthony, believed that good people who do good jobs always win regardless of discriminatory hurdles.

SUMMARY

This chapter analyzed the experiences of black immigrants with regard to achieving the American dream as defined by James Truslow Adams. Our study participants reported that their lives had been better and richer mostly because they had become self-reliant, hardworking, and open-minded. Also, the social structure in the United States has helped them achieve economic success. However, their social lives had been incomplete for the most part, as they missed their homelands, families, friends, and special occasions. They used different means to minimize the void of not having family and friends in the host country. They talked to the loved ones remotely and traveled home to visit.

The chapter also showed that black African immigrants felt that they had not been fully accepted in America and had been discriminated against in different ways. To overcome these challenges, respondents devised strategies that helped them to either minimize the obstacles or refuse to accept the roadblocks as such. Some of the strategies they used to overcome biases and discriminatory treatment, such as patience, perseverance, and avoidance are more instrumental. In fact, poverty and limited educational and employment advancement opportunities push immigrants out of their homelands. Hence, knowing the reasons for migrating, one may endure challenges, even discrimination, in order to reach one's goal. Also, many black African immigrants may already have been aware of the lot of native-born black or African Americans prior to migrating. Furthermore, these immigrants may know about some fashion of biases and discrimination in their homelands. For instance, as reported by Igwe (2009), caste-based or discrimination based on ethnic affiliation exists in Africa. All of the aforementioned factors may make black immigrants oblivious and/or less reactive to discrimination.

Chapter Four

Migrating Out of the United States

Voluntary migrants, especially economic migrants who come to the United States, do so in order to better their lives. However, not all of these immigrants permanently stay in the United States. Some eventually end up returning to their countries of origin or move elsewhere. The selectivity factors of migration which explain why certain people leave their countries of origin and settle in a different country also explain why some immigrants move out of their host countries and return to their home countries (Reagan and Olsen, 2000). For instance, Gmelch (1980) and Cerase (1974) described a typology of immigrants who return to their home countries. Cerase's classification of returned Italian migrants fell into four categories: 1. return of failure: this represents people who were unable to overcome challenges in the host country; 2. return of conservatism: refers to immigrants who could not forget about returning to their homeland while they were in the host country; 3. return of innovation: describes immigrants who return home in order to improve their homelands with new skills that they have acquired in the host country; and 4. return of retirement: old aged immigrants who return to retire.

Gmelch's typology (1980), which was mainly based on a review of the literature, has three groups of returnees: 1. returnees who did not intend to settle abroad; 2. returnees who intended a permanent stay in the host country but have to return because of necessity; and 3. returnees who wanted to stay permanently but had a change of heart and returned to their home countries. Also, studies have shown that there are push and pull factors that motivate immigrants to return to their homelands. Some scholars reported that unfavorable economic circumstances in host country such as unemployment (Hernandez-Alvarez 1968), desire to be with one's own culture, family and friends (Richardson 1968; Toren 1976), family obligations such as ailing or elderly parents, and, especially for non-white migrants, prejudice and discrimination (Davison 1968) are all factors that have been shown to either push or pull immigrants in or out of the host countries.

Although the aforementioned studies have been conducted decades ago, some contemporary studies have also reported some of these factors that make immigrants return to their home countries. For example, King (2000) classified the causes of migrants returning home in four groups: 1. economic factors (unemployment in host country, prospects of more and/or better jobs in homeland, and desire to invest savings); 2. social factors (racial hostility and/or difficulty of integration, homesickness, and desire for enhanced status); 3. family life cycle (retirement, parental ties, marriage, and children's education); and 4. political (government policy in sending and receiving countries). In a corresponding study, Gibson and McKenzie (2009) reported that family, a personal connection to the home country, and lifestyle were the primary reasons why migrants from Tonga, Papua New Guinea, and New Zealand returned to their home countries.

With regard to the United States, Reagan and Olsen (2000) used national data of 1.5 generations of immigrants to investigate factors associated with return migration. They reported a negative association between duration of residence in America and propensity to out-migrate, a positive correlation between age at the time of immigration and the chances of returning to one's home country, and a negative association between one's market value in America and the decision to return.

This chapter discusses black African-born Americans' views on moving back to Africa or elsewhere. Our study participants were asked if they had ever considered giving up the American dream and migrating out of the United States. Also, they were asked to provide explanations for either considering migrating out of or staying in the United States. Over half of the participants (55%) had considered returning to their home countries, 6% had considered migrating to Europe, and the rest (39%) stated that they had never considered migrating out of the United States. This chapter discusses the findings within the framework of transnationalism.

TRANSNATIONALISM AND BLACK AFRICAN IMMIGRANTS

The concept of transnationalism has generated some debate because of its definition and applications (Waldinger and Fitzgerald, 2004; Vertovec 2004). However, broadly defined, immigrant transnationalism refers to the various global and/or cross-national activities in which immigrants regularly engage (Lima 2010). While immigrants have always had ties with both their countries of origin as well as their host countries, today's migrants are heavily engaged in the processes of maintaining and promoting activities and ties between their home and host countries, and thus are called transnational migrants (Glick Schiller, Basch, and Blanc-Szanton, 1992). Transnational migrants have influence on both home and host countries. They have economic, political, and socio-cultural impacts on these countries (Mahler, 2000; Vertovec, 2004; Portes, Guarnizo and Landolt, 1999).

The many new modes of transportation and communications have made transnationalism possible and strengthened transnational ties among immigrants and their families, friends, as well as social relations, communities, and states (Portes, Guarnizo and Landolt, 1999). Hence, as Levitt (2001) perfectly described it, today's immigrants are able to use advances in communications and transportation systems to be involved in the daily activities and functioning of their home communities in significantly different ways than in the past. For example, international travel that took days, weeks, and at times months to accomplish are now a matter of hours or a couple of days at most. Also, advances in information technologies have made it possible to instantaneously communicate with people across the globe. All these changes have not only improved the lives of immigrants, but also have allowed immigrants to have an impact in multiple places at the same time. Consequently, the notion of space and distance has shrunk.

As the numbers of African immigrants to the United States continue to grow so do the networks, activities, and ideologies they create span national boundaries. For instance, Arthur (2000), Attah-Poku (1996), Diouf (2001), N'Diaye and N'Diaye, 2007) and (Yeboah, 2008) all reported the importance of African immigrant organizations and associations that focus on issues inherent to their lives as immigrants, as well as to their lives in their local communities, towns, and countries they left behind. As these immigrants settle in the United States, they usually do not forget about their homelands. Hence they hold and discuss ideas about development, welfare, and stability for their respective countries of origin. They also create activities such as fundraisers to help their community members in the United States as well as back home. There are many different ways through which the black Africans that we investigated create and maintain their transnational ties in the United Sates. These ties influence their lives in the United States as well.

REASONS FOR WANTING TO MIGRATE OUT

While none of the questions in the interview guide asked about immigrant associations, the topic and functions of associations came up numerous times during data collection. Some of the actual interviews were conducted during regular meeting times of some of the associations. Furthermore, a few participants discussed the goals of their associations and their personal reasons for being members of the associations when they were asked questions about whether or not they ever considered migrating out of America. For instance, Osaze reflected on the accomplishments and goals of his association with regard to people in Nigeria:

> You know, it is not just to have an organization where people can meet, but you want to be able to have impact on the quality of life of Nigerians here and also to see what can be done to help people back home, to affect the condition of living of people in Nigeria who are not so privileged as we are.

This sentiment was echoed by 10% of the respondents, especially those who had thought about returning to their home countries. Conversely, Carlos deplored the non-solidarity among African immigrants and their lack of involvement in collaborative efforts. He confided:

> The truth is we have meetings and meetings, we have groups, but we are not organized in a way where we would, say, be able to discuss and help each other with our challenges and struggles by generating ideas on how to overcome them. We are all professionals, let's do it. Unfortunately we don't. Our community (Africans in America) is very educated. We have PhD, masters, and bachelor's holders but each person becomes selfish [...] If someone does not see what they can get out of an association, they don't come to the meetings. Some people who are here today came because they know it is time this year to have elections. So they want to get a chance to run for the presidency [...].

Some of the respondents often went back to their home country because they were building a house where they would like to eventually retire; others had family members, especially elderly parents, that they regularly visited; still others were trying to set up a business in their home country. As these migrants engaged in the different activities across national boundaries, they also tried to assimilate into the American culture. They learned and adapted to the dominant Anglo-culture as best they could. They all have achieved an American higher education and were working in different sectors in the United States alongside native-born Americans of different racial and ethnic backgrounds. However, some were disenchanted with America because of differences in cultural expectations. Also, because of their transnational ties, they went back and forth to their home countries. Hence, they often compared their lives in America to what they thought their lives could have been in their homelands. Joanna revealed the following when asked if she had considered migrating out of America:

> Yes, if I get a job with the United Nations and I am paid in dollars even if it was slightly less than what I was making, I would go back home because it's stress free. Just like I said it earlier, I use a lot of protective mechanisms here in America. I tell myself, after all, even though this is my adopted country

now, this is America; this is a country that I am a citizen of, but I know that I have somewhere else. I know that I have somewhere else that when I get off the plane, I am treated like a queen, and therefore, I say to myself, okay, let me just give myself some time. If I go back home, I will just be treated as a special person, I am somebody somewhere, even if I am nobody here.

Joanna's comments concurred with Levitt's (2004) observation with regard to ways in which immigrants, especially professionals, use their transnational lives to capitalize on opportunities that both sending and receiving countries have to offer. In fact, Joanna had a good paying job in America, but she used her travels back to her homeland as a way to fight challenges that she experienced in the United States. In general, immigrants who have the means travel to their homelands to reconnect with their culture, family, friends, and community, a process called refueling (Akhtar 1999).

Yenee simply explained why she had thought, on several occasions, about returning to Ethiopia:

Yes, I have often considered giving up the American dream and migrating back to my country of birth just to live a simple life. Instead of work, work, work, school, school, school every day. [...] I would like to go back because you get to live instead of working all the time!

Then she added:

But it doesn't look good on you when you go back there (re-migrating). Because you have this chance to get the American dream, if you go back, people will judge you for coming back. They will be like 'you had the opportunity why are you here?' And it makes sense. There are a lot of people who want to be here in America. But I appreciate it sometimes having this opportunity (living in America). Sometimes that works for me as my motivation, seriously, the fact of being able to be here.

The simplicity of life in Africa, especially in rural areas, was mentioned by other respondents as a primary reason for wanting to migrate out of the United States. However, some would out-migrate only when they retire because they believe they would by then have a better quality of life in their homeland than in America. Abasi commented as follows, "I will not quit, but when I retire I want to be back in Kenya. Life will be easier there. I will not be working. I will live in the countryside which is quieter than in the city. I do not want to die in this country because everybody is back home. I want to be buried in my birthplace. It is not that I hate America, but it is just my wish." Abasi's desire to be "buried at home" would be elaborated on later.

Also, some respondents felt that their Social Security funds will go a long way in Africa compared to America. Maria reported:

Yes, because everything you own here, you have to pay taxes for it. Also, I have seen lots of elderly people crying because they cannot make money because they are no longer working, they are not comfortable anymore. So if I go back to Nigeria, I will be more comfortable. Yes, when I retire I will go back home. I am planning to get my social security money here and use it back home wisely. Here you have to pay taxes for everything including food. In Nigeria, I can manage without having to pay so many bills.

For others, America is the place to be when one is young, but life is better in Africa after one retires. Celine expressed her reasons for eventually returning to Africa:

Yes, I consider moving back to Africa, but I do not want to use the phrase "give up the American dream" and migrating outside the United States because I have not achieved the American dream yet. I am thinking in terms of the future. Me and my husband will go back home after retirement. We love America but it is not a place we want to retire in. When you have money, life is more comfortable in Africa. You do not have to run around to feed yourself. You do not have to worry about going to the nursing home. There will be people to care for us when we are old. You do not have to worry about bills in Africa. It is crazy here in America with bills to pay all the time.

The comments above are not specific to black African immigrants. In fact, return migration has been attributed to preference for country of origin (Hill 1987), differences in cost of living between host and home country, and especially the purchasing power of pensions and savings for retirees (Dustmann 2001). As foreign-born migrants age, they have to make decisions as to whether or not they would age in place or return to their homelands. These decisions are usually made in a rational way considering what is to gain and what is to lose if one decides to age in a host country or move back to the home country. Moreover, evidence suggests that retirement migration is also occurring among native-born Americans whereby retirees are migrating out of the United States and establishing new homes in low-income countries because of financial reasons and improvement of quality of life (Sunil, Rojas and Bradley 2007).

Another source of disappointment was primarily social as some respondents felt they had not been fully accepted in the United Sates because they had been treated unjustly. A few respondents did not think they had advanced socio-economically. Thus they had at times questioned their decision of migrating to the United States. Imani did not mince her words by giving a detailed account of her reason for wanting to return to Ethiopia:

I definitely don't want to age here. I want to go back. You don't even know your neighbors' names. What happens to you if for instance you close your door and then if you die? If you don't have a family who is going to check on you in this country? Really, I don't have any plans to age and die in America. I want to migrate back to Ethiopia because that is my home.

When asked if the United States was not considered as her home, she then replied:

Oh no! They (white Americans) don't consider us to be American regardless of how much you try, you are always a foreigner. I will never feel that America is my home. [...] I discussed this with my husband. These white Americans took over someone else's country. This is really not their country. And especially after Obama got elected it makes you really see the true color of the people you work with. Because it has never happened in the past where a black person got elected in America, you assumed that they are fine with you for being black. And when the black president was elected, they were upset, irritated. They were cussing. The whole political part of it is, they were like, he does not know what he is doing. I don't think Bush was any different than he is. Before, people did not even talk about politics, now they are sitting and talking about the black president. It makes me feel like 'this is what you think about us?'

Mrs. Djoa was also among those who thought America had not treated them right. She commented about her feelings:

Yes, sometimes! My experiences at work make me think about returning to my motherland, back to Africa. At this age and with my qualification, I expected to have been much higher on the social class ladder. Also, one of the instances where I actually have considered going back to Africa was when I went back home and saw one of my mates and saw how well she was doing in business. I thought, well, have I wasted my time by coming to America? Here, it just seems like I am stagnant.

Because of their transnational lives, immigrants may not feel that their host country is home. The notion of home is often attributed to the country of origin among immigrants because it gives them a "sense of continuity and connection with the past and present cultural contexts that foster psychological adjustment" (Tummala-Narra 2009). Additionally, since they have the ability to return to their homelands, immigrants may be reminded of what they may have gained or missed by migrating in the first place. Just like Mrs. Djoa, some immigrants may conclude that immigration was not worthwhile when they compare themselves to people in their home country who did not migrate.

Another concept, "to be buried home," was commonly evoked by other respondents. Some respondents wanted to die and or be buried at home because of cultural practices and convictions. Some wanted to be buried in their homelands because they would like to be with their relatives who have passed on. Others wanted to follow their cultural norms, such as one that requires first-born children to be buried at home. Carlos described why he knew he will not permanently live in the United Sates. He stated:

> Yes, I have considered going back home and I know that being the first born son in my family, I am not going to die in America. I know that even though I am a U.S. citizen, I will not die in America; and even if I die in America, my remains will be taken home because of my culture. I am the first born child of my family and there is nothing that will make me remain in America. I may maintain two residences because my children and things like that. However, I am an African first even though I am an American.

In fact, being buried in one's homeland had both cultural and spiritual significance in the sense that burying the dead in the ancestral land allows one to be in the company of her/his ancestors and join forces with the dead to protect and support the living (Attah-Poku 1996). This belief may be more strongly held by some Africans compared to others, depending on ethnic and cultural convictions and identities.

As indicated by Cerase (1974), Gmelch (1980), and others, different factors influence return migration. However, as reported by Peil (1995), African immigrants prefer to return to their home countries after retirement instead of a permanent stay in their host countries. This fact has also been reported among Senegalese immigrants in Italy (Sinatti 2011). In general, return migration is intimately related to the objectives that guided one's migration decisions in the first place. For instance, some migrants never anticipated permanently staying in their host country (Orowolo 2000). Hence, these migrants will likely return when the moment is right for them. A few study participants fell into this category of immigrants who had planned to stay in the United States for a certain number of years and then return to their homelands. Agatha commented when asked if she had ever thought about migrating out of America:

> Oh yes, oh yes, the reasons why we left Nigeria in the first place was because of my family domestic concerns. We had young kids we were trying to bring up. That's number one, and the other thing was the condition of things in Nigeria. Because when we were leaving in 1978, it was not to settle permanently here in the United States. It was just we thought to live in America for 5 or 10 years, and things will improve at least the education system will improve in Nigeira. So I thought I would return and my kids would eventually have a good education. But unfortunately, things have been going down, and down, and down, day after day. Then we kept saying it would get better tomorrow, but it has not been materialized. So these are some of the realities that we face. You talk to 90% of Africans here in America, they will tell you that they did not come to America to stay, their idea was to come here and eventually go back. I don't know that many Africans who say that their idea was to come here and settle permanently.

For others, life challenges such as changing jobs, and life experiences such as accumulation of new skills in the United States, made them think about migrating out of the United States. Mark revealed:

> Yes, there are times when frustration sets in, in terms of, you know, social pressures and every once in a while, you go through ups and downs. And since you are foreign-born, in my mind you have an alternative, you know! If things are going bad, you would want to set sight on something or someplace else, and for me my home country where I was born was the place I set my mind on.

Then he added the following to show the difference between alternative choices that a native-born and a foreign-born have, highlighting the transnational ties of immigrants:

> Like anybody else, for instance American-born persons might have some situations where they might want to move from one state to another. In my case, instead of moving from one state to another, I think about moving from one country to another country which is from the United States to Ghana. It crossed my mind especially when I was in transition between jobs. Also, I sometimes think if I have this experience and this education, I am more needed in Ghana and in Africa in general because there is a greater need there. And I think it is more fulfilling there as well.

The concept "fulfilling" had been used quite often whenever participants compared their lives in the United States to what they thought their lives will be in their countries of origin. This may represent what Aranda (2007: 217) defined as "strong attachment" to homeland and "weak attachment" to host country among people who experienced relocations.

Olubami also was among those who believed they had accumulated enough skills and knowledge that were more needed in Africa. He believed that he had acquired all that was possibly in his reach. He shared:

> Yes, all the time, all the time; but I won't call it "giving up the American dream." I have a house in Nigeria. I have a car in Nigeria. That's a Nigerian dream by itself. Now, I have gone to a point where I can run for office in Nigeria, and I can have my publishing company too. I could teach and impart knowledge. I've reached a point here in America where my paycheck no longer increases. For example, I am not the head of my department. However, the head of my department does not earn significantly more than me. His salary is only $800 more than mine. I can get $800 just by sewing. So it's easy. So even if I get his job, it's not that much of improvement for me in terms of salary. This country has its plateau. So the best thing is now go back to a college in Nigeria and teach. I can teach them how to write a thesis in the shortest amount of time, I can impart my knowledge to them. I need to give back.

The prospects of economic development in their homelands triggered in a few participants the desire to return to their homelands. Thus, their experiences in America have been shaped by whatever economic changes have been taking place in their homelands (Teo 2011), another characteristic of transnational migrants. Reginald explained:

> Yes, I have considered going back home when we heard that there is prospect of oil in Ghana. We said if things get better back home that would be the best place to be because you would be recognized for what you are and then for what you have achieved. The social status would be better too.

Only one respondent, Kuma, wanted to return to his homeland to help solve family problems. He believed returning would be the best solution although he considered his life fuller because he had not been entangled with these family problems, as he stated in chapter 3. Kuma confided:

> Yes, the reason for me wanting to go back home is family problems at home. I have 8 siblings and most of us are living abroad. However, the way I see things going on, if I go on to stay here for the whole of my life, a lot of things in the family in Ghana are going to fall apart. So if not because of the family problems back in Ghana, I will have to stay here.

While this respondent did not give details of the kind of problem his family had in Ghana, as reported by Mahler (1999) solving family issues across national borders was at times very stressful among Salvadorans in America. This is another way in which immigrants become transnationally engaged with their families that they leave behind.

Before discussing the reasons given by respondents who did not consider returning to their homelands, a point needs to be made. Most of the participants specified that their desire to return to their countries of origin had nothing to do with their views or feelings about the United States. As a matter of fact, most of them used words such as "like" and "love" to describe their feelings toward America, as shown in some of the comments in this chapter. Nevertheless, they believed that the United States did not and could not provide them all their cultural, economic, and social needs. This seemingly ambivalent position of the black African immigrant is shared by other groups of immigrants who have ties to more than one place (Aranda 2007; Teo 2011).

REASONS FOR NOT WANTING TO MIGRATE OUT

Thirty-nine percent of study participants stated that they had never thought about migrating out. The positions of these immigrants were quite different from the group that wanted to return to Africa. For some, America was the place to be because of the economic opportunities that it offered. For others, their family situations did not permit them to return. Still others thought one could have a positive impact on countries and people regardless of location.

Tariq believed that there are opportunities in the United States and he had not yet achieved the American dream. He revealed:

> No, I am still stretching forward to achieve the American dream. Like I said at the beginning, America is a land of opportunities and I would not trade this for any other place, I have not travel elsewhere, but I believe this is a true land of opportunities.

Just like Tariq, Alfred from Ghana also believed that America was a unique nation and had a lot to offer people. He explained:

> No, I had not considered migrating out of America. You know, as long as there is no other country that is as aspiring and as good as the United States, I have not had that desire of migrating out of the United States.

Darweshi also made the following remarks focusing on his current family situation:

> No, Kenya does not have these many opportunities. Also, I have a family, now I look at my life not just as an individual, but I look at my wife and children. My wife is American and my kids were born here. So my life is not that simple in a way that I say I will pick up my stuff and leave America.

Abeba elaborated on the reasons for not wanting to return to her homeland by emphasizing her national and transnational ties in both her home and host countries:

> Never thought about that! I am happy here. My kids are American. Lot of people think that when they retire, they will go back home. Of course I grew up there (Ethiopia). I have lots of friends, cousins, and relatives there. Yes, I would go back there to visit. But when people tell me that they will return to their home country, I tell them we will see. Because my kids are here, they will get married here; my grand-kids will be here. How will I be able to live back home while they are here? Probably, I might want to go there once or twice a year if I can afford it, but I don't think I would go back and stay. A lot of immigrants think that way (returning to their home country), but I doubt it. I have never seen people leave for good. They go there, stay there for six months and come back again. It depends on one's financial situation as well. I don't want to be away from my kids and I don't think my kids will like living there.

Abeba was right when she said that she "had never seen people leave for good." In fact, this has been an issue faced by some immigrants who return to their homelands. Some return to the host country after living in the home country for a while because of difficulties that they experienced re-adjusting to the culture and lifestyle of their country of origin. This was the situation that Bandela faced when he returned to Nigeria. He disclosed the following when he was asked if he had ever considered migrating out, "Yes, I have tried. I actually returned to Nigeria. The problem is that it was difficult to adjust to a new place because I stayed in America for too long, so it was difficult to live in any other society or country. I have been away from Nigeria for too long."

Akim had never thought about migrating back to his homeland because he did not see the need to do so. He used an ideology that his mother instilled in him to explain his view:

> No, I had never considered migrating out of America, you know what? My mother left this message with me and it is still in my head. She said that I belong to the world, and that I can serve anywhere. It could be in Nigeria, it could be in America. Mandela is in South Africa, but the whole world knows about him. Michael Jackson was in the United States, but the whole world knew about him. So I can be anywhere and contribute to the world. [...] So as far as I'm concerned, I can sit in this place and help out anywhere in Africa or somewhere else.

Akim's comment touched on globalization, a process of interaction and integration of people, corporations, and nations. The effects of globalization have intensified just as transnationalism has intensified because of present day technologies. Thus, as Akim stated, one can reach and help people regardless of one's place of residency, a core concept of transnationalism.

SUMMARY

This chapter has examined reasons why some black African-born immigrants in Texas, from a transnational perspective, had considered returning to their homelands while others had not. Factors such as differences in cultures, prospects of economic development in one's home country, cultural or personal wishes such as being buried in one's place of birth, as well as retirement expectations influenced the desire for return migration. Some scholars have discussed these factors. For instance, those who would out-migrate when they retire are referred to as return of retirement by Cerase (1974). Others who would return to their homelands in order to impart new knowledge and skills that they had acquired in the United States would be referred to as return of innovation. However, black African immigrants who did not want to return to their homelands had children and spouses who were American-born, did not think there was another nation with opportunities as exist in the United States, or could not re-adjust to the culture and lifestyle of their birthplace.

Because of their transnational lives, participants in this study at times presented seemingly ambivalent views of their experiences in the United States. These experiences shaped their identities and perceptions of the future for their American-born children, topics that are discussed in the next chapter. However, a point needs to be made here. The reported views of the black African immigrants with regard to migrating out of the United States were what they believed at the time of the study, though these views could change at any time. Hence, it would have been more appropriate to follow them longitudinally in order to ascertain the changes, if any.

Chapter Five

Future of American-Born Children of Black African-Born Immigrants

The experiences of immigrants in host countries as well as beliefs and values that these immigrants bring with them generally influence how they raise their children and the expectations that they hold about their children's future. The context of reception (defined as ways immigrants are accepted and treated in the host country as well as opportunities that are available to them, as in Portes and Rumbaut, 2006) also has significant impact on how immigrants define themselves and the identity that emerges from the self-definition process (Stepick and Stepick, 2009). This chapter focuses on what the participants of our study thought of the future of children of black African immigrants who were born in the United States. These children, by virtue of the U.S. Constitution, are native-born Americans. Participants' views were inextricably linked with their own diverse experiences in both their home and host countries. These experiences were characterized by their feelings of marginalization in both the United States and their homelands, and their processes of ethnic identification which were principally Afro-centered. Nearly all of the participants thought children born by black African immigrants would have a bright future and would face fewer challenges compared to their own challenges, which were mostly attributed to their foreign-born status and culture. They also believed that their American-born children would have the potential to reach any socioeconomic and political heights they would desire.

Marginalization has been used in different contexts by different investigators in sociology, economics, and other fields as well. However, the theory of marginal man, developed by Park (1928), refers to a feeling of not belonging to any one particular society/culture. Park, a prominent figure in American sociology, devised and elaborated on the concept of marginality which focused on the lives of groups who are "on the fence, always apart, never integrated" (Smith 1980, 78). In fact, people who are marginalized are not accepted into society because they are considered to be different. Because native-born people tend to hold prejudices and stereotypes against immigrant groups, immigrants are therefore considered marginalized. Also, differences in socioeconomic statuses between native-born Americans and immigrants, especially those in the lower social strata, enhance the differences between native-born and foreign-born people since these immigrants, generally, live separate lives in relation to their native-born American counterparts. However, as shown by Weisberger (1992), not only are immigrants unable to completely integrate into the dominant culture, they are unable to fully readjust to their original culture as well. Consequently, immigrants experience double ambivalence. They vacillate between their native and host cultures without wholeheartedly belonging to either, thus having no roots.

There are some characteristics of immigrants that are worth noting. Immigrants have different identities in order to fully function in either society. Being able to possess multiple identities is considered as asset, a social capital that allows today's immigrants to efficiently function regardless of the society in which they find themselves (Trueba 2002). They also develop a collective conscience that stems from their experiences of marginalization. As described by Brodwin (2003), whatever collective identity that a marginal group develops, it is in response to the political experiences of the place where they reside because this identity is negotiated and constructed based on the social contexts that they live in (Ali and Sonn, 2010; Bhatia 2002; Deaux 2006).

Today's immigrants are also diasporic more than ever, and, as diasporic groups, they go through a process of collective identity development as they experience the tension of "living here and remembering/desiring another place" (Clifford 1997, 255). Also, immigrants in a new country usually undergo a process of acculturation during which ethnic identity becomes a potent experience whereby they develop a subjective sense of belonging to a group or a culture (Phinney, Horenczyk, Liebkind, and Vedder, 2001). Immigration affects the identity process of immigrants in other ways as well (Kadianaki, 2010; Aveling and Gillespie, 2008; Howarth 2002). Immigrants in their foreign-lands have to negotiate their ethnic identity through a redefining and recreating process which occurs during daily interaction in different social contexts (Nagel 1994; Verkuyten and Wolf, 2002). Hence, the process of ethnic identity is a social outcome; ethnic identity emerges out of social interaction.

The development of ethnic identity is a complex process that requires immigrants not only to challenge the cultural hegemony of the host country, but also to be able to affirm whatever they deem important about their ethnic identity. It is important to note that ethnic minorities have stronger ethnic identity than white Americans in general (Phinney, Cantu, and Kurtz, 1997). This chapter shows that the views of our study participants regarding the future of American-born children by black African immigrants were driven by their experiences of marginalization and ethnic identity. Furthermore, most of the participants thought that for the most part black American children whose parents are African immigrants would have much better lives than their immigrant parents' lives.

MARGINALIZATION

Most of the participants expressed some feelings of marginalization. Some felt marginalized whenever they went back home to visit, others felt marginalized in the United States. Marginalization in the United States stemmed mainly from the ways American-born people interacted with respondents. Young Ethiopian immigrants were among those who especially reported being marginalized in the United States as noted in the following remarks.

Imani described how people at her workplace and some of her African American friends set her aside as a person who is different from them, and hence who was unable to understand the intricacies of American society. She recounted some of her experiences:

> The moment you open your mouth they treat you differently because you don't speak like them because of your accent. You go to a meeting and maybe a person may think you are African American; however, the minute you start speaking and they hear your accent, then they begin to treat you differently. Absolutely, I have been treated differently. They back off. They think you don't understand their world. I see the interaction they have with other African Americans (native-born blacks) or the interaction they have had with me before I started to speak. The minute you start speaking they are like, oh, she is different, she is not one of us. Even my friends, I have some African American friends who will be like oh you won't understand. Why would I not understand? Yes, I am not originally from here, but it does not mean that I don't understand your world. At the end of the day, it is the same life. They did not live through slavery. Yes, they are discriminated against, so am I because I am female, I am black, and I am not from this country originally. I have three things against me, but I try not to think about that. You definitely feel that you are not part of their group sometimes.

Dawit also explained his feelings of not being fully accepted through the ways people viewed and treated him in general. He shared:

> It is just a feeling. You could be in a room and you might feel out of place. Sometimes it is verbal, like people make negative comments or jokes about your race and place of origin, especially when you are African. This girl I was recently dating told me that whenever she saw skinny people she would say,

"Oh, you look like Ethiopian" and this was not a compliment because in America skinny is good but she had a negative connotation to it because when she met me and met my friend then she said "wow, Ethiopians are beautiful." When she told me about that, my reaction was that this is what people think of Ethiopians. I have people say to me numerous times, "Oh man! how is it like in Ethiopia?" The only thing people know from Ethiopia was from Michael Jackson's song "We are the World."

As expressed by participants and shown in the two illustrative comments above, American people did not fully accept African-born immigrants because they viewed them as different in terms of their culture, their ways of speaking English (accent), and place of origin. Also, native-born Americans considered participants culturally incompetent. This transpired in the ways these foreign-born Africans were treated in their daily interactions with native-born Americans. For instance, a phrase from Imani's description of her interactions with her American fellows proves the point: "Oh, you won't understand." Because these immigrants were not originally from America, people assumed that they were culturally unable to understand the experiences of American-born people. This, along with other assumptions and interactions, ultimately gave participants a sense of not belonging to American society, a core characteristic of a marginal person. Additionally, an important point made by participants was captured by Dawit's comments about people making negative comments and jokes with regard to one's race and place of origin, especially toward people who come from Africa. This idea was conveyed throughout the interviews. In fact, the media portrayal of Africa does not help either since most often Africa is represented as a disease, poverty, corruption, and violence ridden continent. According to Corces (2009), these are the images that most Westerners have of Africa.

Marginality to homeland was produced by the fact that immigrants had lived and spent so many years in the United States. Thus, they were unable to relate to the culture of the homeland. Also, people in their country of origin viewed them more as Americans because of some of the new behaviors that these immigrants had developed. As Carlos confided below, the sentiment of marginalization created a feeling of emptiness, a void that immigration has produced in the lives of some participants:

I am the first born of my family. Every time I go home to visit, I am like a stranger within my homeland. I play golf and when I go to the golf course, people will say, oh, the American is here because it took me so long to go back home to visit. And it is like, you know, I have been in America for 20 something years and I have been home only five times for an average of one month per visit, thus five months in total. I mean every five years or so, I go home to visit. So I don't have the constant connection with people back home as much as I would prefer. My father is getting old and I myself am in the middle age now. The transition that happens from one generation to another is not relevant in my case. Now I have three sons, none of them have been to my homeland yet to meet their great uncles, aunts and all their cousins there. So there is that emptiness there that I personally feel.

Some of Carlos's experiences, like other immigrants,' exemplified another aspect of the lives of transnational people: because they no longer lived in their original societies, they would not experience the traditional transmission of culture and values that occurs from one generation to the next. Also, their American-born offspring will miss out on these traditional practices. While this may not be considered important for some, others like Carlos grieve over the lack of these practices. However, for other respondents, the importance of teaching these values to their American-born children could neither be compromised by migration nor distance. Hence they made every effort to instill these values to their children in the United States. This is indicated by Kofi's comments when asked about the future of children born by black African immigrants:

I will talk about my own children first and the way I am training them. I try to raise them the way I was raised back home by my parents. But of course, they got the culture of this country. So they will not be fully African, but at least they will have my basics. I have always tried to press my basics into their lives. I am sure they will turn out to be good kids compared to American kids.

Then when asked why he thought it was necessary to teach his children "the basics" that he had from home, he stated:

Because I strongly believe that African values are of high standard compared to American values. Just when you look at the kids and even some parents in this country, the way they raise their kids that is not the way I would like to raise my children.

Some of these immigrants in our study showed a strong sense of Afrocentrism in describing the importance of instilling African values in their American-born children. Also, they believed that their children's knowledge of their African roots is necessary because knowing such roots will keep them grounded. Respondents described such beliefs by emphasizing their ethnic identity.

ETHNIC IDENTITY

Ethnic identity refers to how people conceive and socially identify themselves by primarily focusing on their membership in a particular ethnic group (Gay, 1987). This is an important dimension of one's concept of self because people who ethnically identify with a certain ethnic group draw knowledge, values, and meanings from the group. Furthermore, ethnic identity, which may be taken for granted prior to one's immigration experiences, becomes a salient aspect of one's self in a host country. African immigrants that we interviewed showed some degree of African ethnic identity, although participants spoke more emphatically of their African identity and its roles than others. For instance, Afaafa noted the following when asked about the kind of future she envisioned for American children of black African immigrants:

> To be honest, when I think about if I ever have kids, I would want to take them back to Ethiopia. I know it sounds crazy, but we are at a point where even the education, if you can afford it, you can get the best quality education for your kids in Ethiopia [this statement was to indicate progress of development in some area]. That's the reason we are here. We are not here because we hate our country. No, it's just there are better opportunities here. If I am successful now and do well for myself, I will be at the point that I can afford good life there [in Ethiopia]. I can then take my kids back and teach them the culture because that matters. That's your identity. If you don't know who you are, you will always try to find who you are and you will never achieve anything.

Then when asked why would she want her children to know who they were by taking them to Ethiopia because, after all, they will be born here in America and hence will be Americans, she answered: "I guess they are Americans, but their identity is Ethiopian. Their roots are there, their ancestors were from there."

Afaafa touched on some important aspects of the significance of ethnic identity in one's life, especially people who are members of a stigmatized or a minority group. In fact, research shows that minority people with a strong sense of ethnic identity have higher psychological resiliency (Wong, Eccles, and Sameroff 2003). Also, ethnic identity positively correlates with school attachment, high school completion, and college GPA among African Americans (Chavous, Bernat, Schmeelk-Cone, et al. 2003). Additionally, ethnic identity gives one a secure sense of self (Phinney, Romero, Nava, and Huang 2001; Ong, Phinney, and Dennis 2006; Quintana, 2007).

Another respondent whose comments are worth quoting at length was Beheilu's. He has been in the United States for over two decades. He also emphasized the importance of his African roots, especially his Ethiopian identity, when he explained the significance of instilling African values in his children:

> Africans have pride in their countries. Yes, most people would say: "what do you guys have to be proud of?" but we have pure love and just little things.

When asked about what he meant by "pure love" he then proceeded:

Love for our own people, yes, there is a lot of genocide and this and that that goes on in Africa, but still we are proud of who we are. As an Ethiopian especially, I think this is pretty much the same about other Africans, it does not matter how long you have been here, but for me, I feel like I am first an Ethiopian. It may be what your parents have put in you. I want my kids to have that kind of pride. It does not matter what people say to you. It is not going to get to you. When you look at African Americans here, half of the issues that go on within the African American community is a lack of identity; they have no idea about their roots.

Beheilu believed in the importance of ethnic identity in the lives of African immigrants in general and Ethiopian immigrants in particular. To him, when one is proud of one's ethnic origin, then "It does not matter what people say to you. It is not going to get to you." Indeed, this is so because ethnic identity gives a secure sense of self and, hence, one becomes well grounded.

Furthermore, Beheilu added some comments that touched on race relations in America and some differences between immigrants from Europe (Caucasians) and nonwhite immigrants. He noted:

When Europeans immigrate to America, they don't necessarily want to go back or want their children to go back to their homelands and all of that. I mean, they fit in here at least looks wise. You know, our skin tone does not fit in. That always may be a constant reminder that we don't belong here. The way we talk, the food we eat, the culture we have are all constant reminders that we don't belong here.

As commented by Beheilu above, evidence suggests that ethnic identity has declined and has less importance in the lives of present-day whites (McDermont and Samson 2005; Walters, 1990). However, this was not the case with white immigrants who originally immigrated to the United States a century or so ago. In fact, white immigrants such as Irish, Jewish, and Italians were considered nonwhites and endured prejudices, stereotypes, and discrimination (Allen 1994; Brodkin 1998; Jacobson 1998). Nevertheless, the creation of a white identity eased these challenges for white immigrants (McDermott and Samson 2005). Nonetheless, non-white immigrants and their native-born children are still facing challenges such as discrimination, prejudices, and stereotypes. Because of this fact, some scholars believe that non-whites hold onto their ethnic identity as a protective measure, as it also gives them a secured sense of self.

FUTURE OF AMERICAN CHILDREN BORN BY BLACK AFRICAN IMMIGRANTS

Almost all the participants were optimistic about the future of children born by black African immigrants. Most reported that these children will have better lives than their own because they will easily fit into American society. Others believed that with hard work these children will be able to achieve whatever they want because of all the opportunities that are available to them in the United States. Immani commented about her daughter's future:

> I think they are going to have better opportunities. My daughter is four. It is a better generation. I think they are mixed together well. They don't have to go through what we went through. Like learning our accent, trying to speak like Americans (meaning with non-American accent), they will fit better. But as far as learning the two cultures, they will lose the culture of their parents. They will become more American.

Fitting in was the most recurring theme that respondents used to describe a difference in the lives of the American-born children of black African immigrants. These children will fit in because they did not have the cultural background of their parents and hence their English and behaviors will not set them apart as different. They will evaluate themselves and will be evaluated by other people as American-born, contrary to their parents. These points were reiterated in the following quote. Laura also explained what the future of American-born children of black African immigrants would be like by comparing the situation of immigrants in the United States to those in Europe. She noted:

> They are Americans. They will be the same as Americans. That is one thing that I like. They are born here. When I tell my kids that they are Africans, the say, "no, you are from Africa. I am American, I am from Texas." So, they have the same opportunity like everyone else. They can be president, they can be senator, they can be anything they want to be. They can be doctors or lawyers, or anything. They will get opportunity that we did not get. I wasted a lot of years going here and there. I could not finish school back home because of different situations. They are not going to have that problem. They will finish school and do whatever they want. The best thing that I like about America is that it is fair. I have friends and relatives in Europe. They can be naturalized, but they always ask them: "when are you going back? Are you going to be here forever?" But here, nobody tells you such things. Even when I was not a citizen, nobody even knew that I was not a citizen. Everybody treats you like you are an American. So that is what I like. Nobody cares about your color and nationality. I am proud to be an American and I feel glad that my kids will have a better life than mine.

As stated by Laura and also discussed in Chapter 3, some of the respondents appreciated the fact that they were able to improve their education in the United States, something that they would not have been able to do had they stayed in their home countries. The freedom that immigrants have in the United States, not being constantly jeered by others because of one's foreign-born status, was also something that some participants found very attractive.

The idea of hard work also emerged when participants discussed the future of their children. In general, respondents believed that children who work hard will be more successful than those who do not. Charles commented:

> Compared to what we have, I think they will have a better life. If they work hard, they will have a better life. I did not have the opportunity that they have in terms of schooling. The more they study, the better their life will be. But those kids who just want to sit back, those who are lazy, will suffer.

Mutoni shared how the mixture of two backgrounds—an immigrant background and American background—helps children of immigrants achieve success. To him, because these children have both worlds and know the struggles that come from being immigrants, they would excel at all costs. He explained:

> Very bright, because they have an opportunity to live both worlds. Kids born here by immigrants parents, they have the most potential because they have both worlds. For example, some of the richest billionaires in the United States are immigrants or children of immigrants. They might not necessarily be African immigrants, but they have immigrant connection. The pain is the motivating factor and succeeding, having opportunity, and pain is a perfect mix. I think our children have all the potential to make it.

When asked what he meant by pain, then he elaborated:

> Not pain in the literal sense. I could have used a better word. I mean, suffering, knowing where your parents are from, being able to connect with where your parents are from, and knowing that you grew up in America, you will want to make the situation better. You don't want to be in America and live as if you were in Africa!

SUMMARY

This chapter has discussed how black African-born immigrants viewed the future of their America-born children. First, respondents compared their lives and opportunities or lack thereof in their homelands to opportunities and the lives of their children in the United States. Second, although these participants had some difficulties in America, especially Ethiopian immigrants, they mostly attributed these to their foreign-born status and culture. Ethiopian immigrants may be viewed more negatively because images of famine and poverty in Africa most often come from Ethiopia. However, our study participants mostly had very optimistic views of their children's futures. Some even believed that they and their American children are better off compared to immigrants in some of the European countries where have been continually unaccepted.

However, it is important to mention that although respondents had great hope for the future of their children, studies have shown that some contemporary immigrant children are in dire situations where they lag begin their native-born counterparts in socioeconomic and social indicators (Child Trends 2010; Mather 2009). Unlike our study participants who were all college-educated, middle class people, these children come mainly from working class and poor immigrant families. In addition, although respondents were relatively better off socio-economically, their lives were not devoid of racial and cultural challenges.

Chapter Six

Future of Black African Immigrants and the American Dream

Although African immigrants represent a small proportion of immigrants that are admitted in the United States, their numbers have been significantly growing since the passage of the 1965 Immigration and Nationality Act. From a low of 101,520 African-born immigrants in 1980, the estimated number of immigrants from Africa was 1,023,363 in 2007 (Reed and Andrzejewski 2010). Also, their duration of residence in the United States is relatively short as most immigrated since 1990 (Terrazas 2009). Additionally, over 35% of adult African immigrants have a bachelor's or higher degree (Mason and Austin 2011; Terrazas 2009). However, evidence suggests that black African immigrants earn, on average, significantly less than their white African counterparts, as well as native-born American workers and other immigrants (Dodoo and Takyi 2002; Moore, Amey, and Bessa 2009). With positive attributes, such as high levels of education, which are valued and highly remunerated in the market place, one may wonder why black African immigrants have a discrepancy between their educational achievements and earnings attainments.

This book set out to investigate whether or not black African immigrants in Texas are achieving the American dream, using James Truslow Adams' definition: "... the American dream, that dream of a land in which life should be better and richer and fuller for every man, with opportunity for each according to his ability or achievement. ... It is not a dream of motor cars and high wages merely, but a dream of a social order in which each man and each woman shall be able to attain to the fullest stature of which they are innately capable, and be recognized by others for what they are, regardless of the fortuitous circumstances of birth or position" Adams (1931, 404). This book hoped to uncover some of the factors that may explain the educational attainment and earnings discrepancy. Hence it examined the achievement of the American dream by black African immigrants from its materialistic characteristic to the moralistic aspect. It also discussed the challenges that these immigrants faced and ways they tried to overcome them. Furthermore, the book discussed the views of black African immigrants with regard to migrating out of the United States and the future of American-born children whose parents migrated from Africa to the United States.

Several factors explain the decision to migrate among black African immigrants that we studied. While some came for American higher education, others immigrated to reunite with family. A few came to seek refuge or asylum. Life in the host country, the United States, was at first challenging as these immigrants had to learn the American way of life. Most of the respondents had difficulty adjusting to the American culture and expectations upon their arrival, but were able to acculturate with time. However, a few were still struggling with the American culture and expectations, even at the time of the study. Those who immigrated when they were young experienced more culture shock, but have been able to quickly adjust to American culture.

Almost all of the study participants considered America as a land of opportunity because of the American exceptionalist character whereby hard work usually leads to material success (Jillson 2004). Specifically, the black African immigrants in Texas thought that America is a land of opportunity because America offers its residents an opportunity to further education regardless of age and social class. Student loans, grants, and scholarship opportunities were mentioned as the means to reach one's potential in education. Also, amenities such as security, infrastructure, and law and order were considered part of the opportunities that America offers. However, a few respondents doubted that America is a land of opportunity because, in reality, America is a land of consumerism and work excess which oftentimes are detrimental to one's life.

Additionally, most of the black African immigrants' definitions of the American dream focused on the material aspect as participants discussed all the material goods they have been able to secure in the United States. However, a few revealed that the American dream is ironically the "American nightmare" because in order to achieve the dream, one has to undergo significant stressors that affect one's health and life as well as the welfare of one's family. The study participants mostly reported that they had not achieved the American dream because they had fallen short of their goals such as getting a certain degree or certification, owning a business, or obtaining a certain professional position. While some identified personal factors such as having children, which slowed them down and distracted them from reaching their goals, others believed that external factors such as biases (prejudices, stereotypes, and discrimination) were to blame. Still others reported that coming from a different culture and the inability to fully understand the American culture were the primary reasons for not achieving their American dream.

Despite these roadblocks, study participants reported that the United States had been good to them by making them become better people. Some had changed their ways of doing things, which consisted of relying on others to serve them, to becoming self-reliant. Others had also become open-minded. They thought America had made their lives richer by providing them all the material goods such as jobs, houses, vehicles, and freedom to do whatever they wanted as long as they did not break any laws. Also, some appreciated the American meritocratic system whereby their efforts were rewarded accordingly. However, our study participants also reported that their lives in the United States had been, at best, incomplete. They missed their families and friends and special occasions and holidays. They also encountered other challenges which mainly reflected the moralistic aspect of the definition of the American dream. They reported experiences such as not being fully accepted by native-born Americans in general and in particular by white Americans, being discriminated against, and being unappreciated. In fact, all of these challenges created a sense of marginalization among respondents. They felt unwelcomed in America. Some respondents also thought that regardless of their duration of residence in the United States, they would always be treated as the "other." They also revealed that they would never be fully accepted. Consequently, some wanted to eventually return to their native countries permanently. Others wanted to out migrate after retirement as they believed that life in their homelands would be much better and less stressful. They also considered the fact that their pension would have a greater purchasing power in their homelands than in America.

Nearly all of the participants believed that children born by black African immigrants would have a bright future and would face fewer challenges compared to their own challenges because these children will be able to fit into American society. They also believed that their American-born children would have the potential to reach any socioeconomic and political heights they would desire. Respondents thought that it was necessary for these children to have an African identity, because knowing where one originates from keeps one grounded.

WHERE DO WE GO FROM HERE?

This study was about black African immigrants who had an American college education and were naturalized citizens. They represent an elite group as their social and economic characteristics afforded them a middle class status. Hence, some of the findings may reflect this unique background that may not be relevant to other poor or working class black African immigrants. For

instance, some of the respondents were reluctant to even accept the possibility of being held back by discriminatory practices. Others used different
labels to describe unfair treatment of which they were victims. While this
study did not investigate lower class or poor African immigrants, Waters
(1994), in her study of second-generation black immigrants, reported an
association between ethnic identification and views on discrimination and
availability of opportunities. Second-generation black children whose self-
identification was black American were likely to view America as having
more racial discrimination and offering limited opportunities to blacks,
whereas those who self-identified as West Indian were likely to see the
United States as fair and rewarding people according to their work. From this
finding, one may wonder if our study participants would differ from their
counterparts from lower socioeconomic classes with regard to how they
viewed discriminatory practices.

   Another point worth noting is the fact that the black immigrants in our
study seemed to have ambivalent views of the United States and what it has
done for them. People who had positive views on some aspects of America
had at the same time negative views when it came to other aspects. As
immigrants often compare their lives in a host country to their lives in their
homeland, they always go through a process of "living here (host country)
and thinking of there (home country)." However, this comparative process
usually is not objective as immigrants not only have to find a new identity in
the host country, but also mourn the loss of family and friends as well as their
culture and familiar things that they have grown accustomed to back in their
homelands (Akhtar 1999). These facts cloud their objectivity. On one hand,
feelings of marginalization may force some immigrants to avoid interacting
with native-born people. Marginalization may increase transnationalism, on
the other hand, as these immigrants find more solace at home whenever they
return. Hence, they may never consider the United States home and eventually will return to their homelands. Return migration has economic costs for
host countries as immigrants usually take home all their savings. This is an
important fact that policy makers should consider with regard to improving
the lives of immigrants in the United States. One way to ease the strains on
immigrants is to create an environment where not only race and ethnicity-
related issues are easily and honestly debated, but also, no one feels pres-
sured to be politically correct. By so doing, both immigrants and native-born
Americans will be able to shares experiences and feelings in a healthy way.
This will create understanding and trust between the two groups.

   One thing that is certain is that more immigrants that will come from
Africa to the United States. Will these immigrants persevere as their prede-
cessors and not react to prejudice and discrimination? Also, black immigrants who are already in the United States will become more knowledgeable

in identifying discriminatory behaviors even when they are covert. Will they still be patient in reacting to the perpetrators of biased behaviors?

As reported by other scholars and mentioned in the introduction, discrimination is still at work in the United States. Policy makers should be aware that non-white immigrants especially still endure unfair treatment from native-born Americans. This may slow their process of assimilating as they know that assimilation may not change their lot.

Appendix

Some questions that were asked of African immigrants (from Ethiopia, Ghana, Kenya, and Nigeria):

1. Can you tell me about your life?
2. What was it like growing up in (country of origin)?
3. What made you want to come to the United States?
4. What year did you come to the United States?
5. How did you manage to get here?
6. How do you find life here?
7. Do you perceive America as a land of opportunity? If so, how? If not, why?
8. When you think of the "American dream" how would you define it?
9. Have you achieved the "American dream"? Why and why not?

   a. What roadblocks have hindered you from achieving the dream?
   b. What things have you tried to overcome these roadblocks?

The participants were given a typed definition of the "American dream" by Adams. I gave them time to think about the definition and then proceeded with the following questions that use some key phrases of the definition of the "American dream."

1. Do you think your life in America has been better compared to your life in (home country)? Why and why not?

   a. What roadblocks have hindered your achieving a better life?

      b. What things have you tried to overcome the roadblocks?

2. Do you think your life in America has been richer compared to your life in (home country)? Why and why not?

      a. What roadblocks have hindered you from achieving a richer life?
      b. What things have you tried to overcome the roadblocks?

3. Do you think your life in America has been fuller compared to your life in (home country)? Why and why not?

      a. What roadblocks have hindered you from achieving a fuller life?
      b. What things have you tried to overcome the roadblocks?

4. Do you think you have attained to the fullest stature of which you are innately capable? Why and why not?

      a. What roadblocks have hindered you from achieving the fullest stature of which you are capable?
      b. What things have you tried to overcome the roadblocks?

5. Do you think America offers you opportunity according to your ability or achievement? Why and why not?

      a. What roadblocks have hindered you from opportunities?
      b. What things have you tried to overcome the roadblocks?

6. Do you think in America people recognize you for what you are regardless of who you are? Why and why not?
7. Have you ever considered giving up the "American dream" and migrating out of the United States? If yes, why? If no, why?
8. If yes, where do you want to migrate to? And why?
9. What kind of future do you envision for American-born children of black African immigrants in the United States? Please explain why.

Bibliography

Adams, Darrell. E. 1997. "Mentoring Women and Minority Officers in the US Military." Research paper presented to the Research Department Air Command and Staff College. Accessed July 01, 2012. http://www.au.af.mil/au/awc/awcgate/acsc/97-0607b.pdf.

Adams, James T. 1931. *The Epic of America*. Boston: Little, Brown, and Company.

Akhtar, Salman. 1995. "A Third Individuation: Immigration, Identity, and the Psychoanalytic Process." *Journal of the American Psychoanalytic Association* 43: 1051-1084.

———. 1999. *Immigration and Identity: Turmoil, Treatment, and Transformation*. Northvale, NJ: Jason Aronson.

———. 1999. "The Immigrant, the Exile, and the Experience of Nostalgia." *Journal of Applied Psychoanalytic Studies* 1(2): 123-130.

Ali, Lütfiye, and Christopher Sonn. 2010. "Constructing of Identity as a Second-Generation Cypriot Turkish in Australia: The Multi-hyphenated Other." *Culture and Psychology* 16(3): 416-436.

Allen T.W. 1994. *The Invention of the White Race*. London: Verso.

Alsop, Christine. 2002. "Home and Away: Self-Reflexive Auto-ethnography." Forum: Qualitative Social Research 3(3), Art. 10. Accessed February 01, 2012. http://www.qualitativeresearch.net/index.php/fqs/article/view/823/1788.

Appadurai, Arjun. 1990. "Disjuncture and Difference in the Global Culture Economy." *Theory, Culture, and Society* 7: 295-310.

Aranda, Elizabeth. 2007. "Struggles of Incorporation Among the Puerto Rican Middle Class." *The Sociological Quarterly* 48: 199-228.

Arthur, John. A. 2000. *Invisible Sojourners: African Immigrant Diaspora in the United States*. Westport: Praeger.

Attah-Poku, Agyemang, 1996. "Asanteman Immigrant Ethnic Association: An Effective Tool for Immigrant Survival and Adjustment Problem Solution in New York City." *Journal of Black Studies* 27(1): 56-76.

Aveling, Emma-Louise and Gillespie, Alex. 2008. "Negotiating Multiplicity: Adaptive Asymmetries within Second-generation Turks' Society of Mind." *Journal of Constructivist Psychology* 21: 1-23.

BBC News. 2011. "Country Profile: Ghana." Accessed June 6, 2011. https://www.cia.gov/library/publications/the-world-factbook/geos/et.html.

———. 2011. "Country Profile: Ghana." Accessed June 6, 2011. http://news.bbc.co.uk/2/hi/africa/country_profiles/1023355.stm.

———. 2011. "Country Profile: Ethiopia." Accessed June 11, 2011. http://news.bbc.co.uk/2/hi/africa/country_profiles/1072164.stm.

————. 2011. "Country Profile: Kenya." Accessed June 11, 2011. http://news.bbc.co.uk/2/hi/africa/country_profiles/1024563.stm.

————. 2011. "Country Profile: Nigeria." Accessed June 11, 2011. http://news.bbc.co.uk/2/hi/africa/country_profiles/1064557.stm.

Behar, Ruth. 1996. *The Vulnerable Observer: Anthropology that Breaks Your Hearts*. Boston: Beacon Press.

Benjamin, Lois. 2005. *The Black Elite: Still Facing the Color Line in the Twenty-first Century*, 2nd ed. New York: Rowman & Littlefield.

Bhatia, Sunil. 2002. "Acculturation, Dialogical Voices, and the Construction of Diasporic Self." *Theory and Psychology 12: 55-77*.

Blancero, Donna, M. and Robert D. DelCampo (2005). "Hispanic in the Workplace: Experiences with Mentoring and Networking." Employment Relations Today 32 (2):31-39.

Blunt, Elizabeth. 2001. "West Africa's Little Maids." BBC News, Monday, April 15, 2001. Accessed January 31, 2012. http://news.bbc.co.uk/2/hi/africa/1279776.stm.

Bonilla-Silva, Eduardo. 1997. "Rethinking Racism." *American Sociological Review* 62 (3):465-480.

————. 2000. "This is a White Country: The Racial Ideology of the Western Nations of the World System." *Sociological Inquiry* 70(2):188-214.

————. 2010. *Racism without Racists: Color-blind Racism and Racial Inequality in Contemporary America*, 3rd ed. New York: Rowman & Littlefield.

Bonilla-Silva, Eduardo, and Tyrone A. Forman. 2000. "I Am Not a Racist but ...": Mapping White College Students' Racial Ideology in the USA." *Discourse and Society* 11(1): 50-85.

————. 2002. "The Linguistics of Color Blind Racism: How to Talk Nasty about Blacks Without Sounding 'Racist.'" Critical Sociology 28:41-64.

Borjas, George J. 1990. *Friends or Strangers: The Impact of Immigrants on the U.S. Economy*. New York: Basic Books.

————. 1999. *Heaven's Door: Immigration Policy and the American Economy*. Princeton: Princeton University Press.

Bourdieu, Pierre. 1977. *Outline of a Theory of Practice*. New York: Cambridge University Press.

Boyd, Monica. 1989. "Family and Personal Networks in International Migration: Recent Developments and New Agendas." *International Migration Review* 23: 638-70.

Bratsberg, Bernt, and James F. Ragan. 2000. "The Impact of the Host-country Schooling on Earnings: A Study of Male Immigrants in the United States." *Journal of Human Resources* 38(1): 63-105.

Bratsberg, Bernt, James F. Ragan, and Zafar M. Nasir. 2002. "The Effect of Naturalization on Wage Growth: A Panel Study of Young Male Immigrants." *Journal of Labor Economics* 20(3): 568-597.

Brint, Steven, and Gerome Karabel. 1989. "American Education, Meritocratic Ideology, and the Legitimation of Inequality: The Community College and the Problem of American Exceptionalism." *Higher Education* 18: 725-735.

Brodkin K. 1998. *How Jews Became White Folks and What That Says about Race in America*. New Brunswick, NJ: Rutgers University Press.

Brodwin, Paul. 2003. "Marginality and Subjectivity in the Haitian Diaspora." *Anthropological Quarterly* 76(3): 383-410.

Brown, Michael K., Martin Carnoy, Elliott Currie, Troy Duster, David B. Oppenheimer, Marjorie M. Shultz, and David Wellman. 2003. *With-washing Race: The Myth of a Color-blind Society*. Berkeley: University of California Press.

Cadwallader, Martin. 1992. *Migration and Residential Mobility: Macro and Micro Approaches*. Madison: University of Wisconsin Press.

Cerase, Francesco P. 1974. "Expectations and Reality: A Case Study of Return Migration from the United States to Southern Italy." *International Migration Review* 8 (2): 245-262.

Chase, Susan. 2003. "Learning to Listen: Narrative Principles in a Qualitative Research Methods Course." *In Up Close and Personal: The Teaching and Learning Narrative Research*, edited by Ruthellen Josselson, Amia Lieblich, and Dan P. McAdams, 79-99. Washington: American Psychological Association.

Chavous, T. M., Bernat, D., Schmeelk-Cone, K., Caldwell, C., Kohn-Wood, L. P., and M. Zimmerman. (2003). "Racial Identity and Academic Attainment among African American adolescents." *Child Development 74*, 1076-1091.

Child Trends. 2010. "Child Trends Indicators." From Child Trends Data Bank. Accessed July 20, 2012. http://childtrendsdatabank.org.

Chiswick, Barry. 1979. "The Economic Progress of Immigrants: Some Apparently Universal Patterns." *In Contemporary Economic Problems*, edited by William Fellner, 359-399. Washington: American Enterprise Institute.

CIA The World FactBook. 2011. "Ethiopia." Accessed May 31, 2011. https://www.cia.gov/library/publications/the-world-factbook/geos/et.html.

———. 2011. "Ghana." Accessed May 31, 2011. https://www.cia.gov/library/publications/the-world-factbook/geos/gh.html.

———. 2011. "Kenya." Accessed May 31, 2011. https://www.cia.gov/library/publications/the-world-factbook/geos/ke.html.

———. 2011. "Nigeria." Accessed May 31, 2011. https://www.cia.gov/library/publications/the-world-factbook/geos/ni.html.

Cilliers, Jackie, Barry Hughes, and Jonathan Moyer. 2011. African Futures 2050: The Next Forty Years. Institute for Security Studies. Monograph 175. Accessed January 04, 2012. http://www.foresightfordevelopment.org/sobi2/Resources/African-Futures-2050-The-Next-Forty-Years.

Clark, William A. V. 2003. *Immigrants and the American Dream: Remaking of the Middle Class*. New York: Guilford Press.

Clifford, James. 1997. *Routes: Travel and Translation in the Late Twentieth Century*. Cambridge, MA: Harvard University Press.

Corces, Laureano. 2009. "When Animals Speak: Staging Representations of Africa." *Afro-Hispanic Review* 28(2): 269-271.

Crevecoeur, J. Hector St. John de. 1782. *Letters From an American Farmer*. New York: Abert & Charles Boni.

Cullen, Jim. 2003. *The American Dream: A Short History of an Idea That Shaped a Nation*. Oxford: Oxford University Press.

Davison, Betty. 1968. "No Place Back Home: A Study of Jamaicans Returning to Kingston, Jamaica." *Race and Class* 9: 499-509.

Deaux, Kay. 2006. *To be an Immigrant*. New York: Russell Sage Foundation.

De Haas, Hein. 2008. "Migration and Development: A Theoretical Perspective." Working Papers 9; International Migration Institute: University of Oxford.

De Jong, Gordon. F. 2000. "Expectations, Gender, and Norms in Migration Decision-making." *Population Studies* 54: 307-319.

Diouf, Sylviane. 2001. "The New African Diaspora." The Schomburg Center for Research in Black Culture." Accessed May 05, 2012 at: http://www.inmotionaame.org/texts/viewer.cfm?id=13_000T&page=1.

Dodoo, Francis N. 1991. "Earnings Differences among Blacks in America." *Social Science Research* 20: 93-108.

———. 1997. "Assimilation Differences among Africans in America." *Social Forces* 76: 527-46.

Dodoo, Francis N., and Baffour Takyi. 2002. "Africans in the Diaspora: Black-white Earnings Differences among America's Africans." *Ethnic and Racial Studies* 25(6): 913-941.

Dovidio, John, and Samuel Gaertner. 1996. "Affirmative Action, Unintentional Racial Biases, and Intergroup Relations." *Journal of Social Issues* 52(4):51-75.

Dustmann, Christian. 2001. "Return Migration, Wage Differentials and the Optimal Migration Duration," IZA Discussion paper Series no. 264, Institute for the Study of labor, Bonn. Accessed May 05, 2012 at: http://ftp.iza.org/dp264.pdf.

Eitzen, Stanley D., and Baca M. Zinn. 2006. *Globalization: The Transformation of Social Worlds*. Belmont, CA: Thomson-Wadsworth.

Elahi, Babek, and Grant Cos. 2005. "An Immigrant's Dream and the Audacity of Hope: The 2004 Convention Addresses of Barack Obama and Arnold Schwarzenegger." *American Behavioral Scientist* 49: 454-465.

Ely, Margot, Margaret Anzul, Teri Friedman, Diane Garner, and Ann McCormack-Steinmetz. 1991. *Doing Qualitative Research: Circles within Circles.* New York: Falmer Press.

Erisman, Wendy, and Shannon Looney. 2007. "Opening the Door to the American Dream: Increasing Higher Education Access and Success for Immigrants." A report by Institute of Higher Education Policy. Washington, D.C. Accessed December 28, 2011. http://www.ihep.org/assets/files/publications/m-r/OpeningTheDoor.pdf.

Esses, Victoria, Lynne Jackson, and Tamara Armstrong. 1998. "Intergroup Composition and Attitudes Toward Immigrants and Immigration: An Instrumental Model of Group Conflict." *Journal of Social Issues* 54(4):699-724.

Firebaugh, Glenn, and Kenneth Davis. 1988. "Trends in Antiblack Prejudice, 1972-1984: Region and cohort effects." *American Journal of Sociology* 94:251-272.

Fisher, Walter R. 1973. "Reaffirmation and Subversion of the American Dream." *Quarterly Journal of Speech* 59(2): 160-167.

Freeman, Lance, and Darrick Hamilton. 2004. "The Changing Determinants of Inter-racial Home Ownership Disparities: New York City in the 1990s." *Housing Studies* 19(3): 301-323.

Furman, Frida. 2005. "The Long Road Home." *Journal of Prevention and Intervention in the Community* 30:91-116.

Gadamer, Hans-Georg .1993. *Truth and Method,* 2nd ed. Translation Revised by Joel Weinsheimer and Donald Marshall. New York: Continuum (Original German version published in 1960).

Gallagher, Charles. A. 2003. "Color-Blind Privilege: The Social and Political Functions of Erasing the Color Line in Post Race America." Race, Gender, and Class 10(4): 22-37.

Gay, Geneva. 1987. *Expressively Black: The Cultural Basis of Ethnic Identity.* New York: Praeger.

Getahum, Solomon A. 2007. *The History of Ethiopian Immigrants and Refugees in America, 1900-2000: Patterns of Migration, Survival, and Adjustment.* New York: LFB Scholarly Publishing LLC.

Gibson, John, and David McKenzie. 2009. "The Microeconomic Determinants of Emigration and Return Migration of the Best and Brightest: Evidence from the Pacific." Center for Global Development, Working Paper number 173. Accessed July 07, 2012: http://econ.worldbank.org/external/default/main?pagePK=64165259&theSitePK=469372&piPK=64165421&menuPK=64166093&entityID=000158349_20090617101215.

Giuliamo, Paola, and Ruiz-Arranz. 2005. "Remittances, Financial Development, and Growth." International Monetary Fund Working Paper. Accessed July 01, 2012. http://www.imf.org/external/pubs/ft/wp/2005/wp05234.pdf.

Glazer, Nathan. 1993. "Is Assimilation Dead?" *Annals of the American Academy of Political and Social Science* 530: 122-136.

Glick Schiller, Nina, Basch, Linda, and Cristina Blanc-Szanton. 1992. *Towards a Transnational Perspective on Migration: Race, Class, Ethnicity and Naturalism Reconsidered.* New York: Academy of Sciences.

Gmelch, George. 1980. "Return Migration." *Annual Review of Anthropology* 9: 135-139.

Gordon, April. 1998. "The New Diaspora-African Immigration to the United States." *Journal of the Third World Studies* 15(1): 79-103.

Gordon, Milton. 1964. *Assimilation in American Life: The Role of Race, Religion, and National Origin.* New York: Oxford University Press.

Greeley, Andrew, and Paul Sheatsley. 1971. "Attitudes Toward Racial Integration." *Scientific American* 222:13-19.

Hawley, Amos H. 1944. "Dispersion versus Segregation: A Propos of a Solution of Race Problems." *Papers of the Michigan Academy of Science, Arts and Letters* 30: 667-674.

Heinen, J. Stephen and Colleen O'Neil. 2004. Managing Talent to Maximize Performance. *Employment Relations Today* 31(2): 67-82.

Hermans, Hubert J. M., and Harry. J. G. Kempen. 1998. "Moving Cultures: The Perilous Problems of Cultural Dichotomies in a Globalizing Society." *American Psychologist* 53: 1111-1120.

Hernandez-Alvarez, Jose. 1968. "Migration, Return, and Development in Puerto Rico." *Economic Development and Cultural Change* 16(4): 574-587.

Hill, John. 1987. "Immigrant Decisions Concerning Duration of Stay and Migratory Frequency," *Journal of Development Economics* 25: 221-234.

Himes, Kenneth. 2007. "Consumerism and Christian Ethics." *Theological Studies* 68(1): 132-153.

Howarth, C. 2002. "'So, you're from Brixton?': The Struggle for Recognition and Esteem in a Multicultural Community." *Ethnicities* 2: 237-260.

Howenstine, Erick. 1996. "Expectations and Reality: Mexican Migration to Washington State." *Migration World Magazine* 24: 1-2.

Hyman, Ilene, Hiwot Teffera, and Girma Tizazu. 2008. "Gender, Violence and Health: Postmigration Changes in Gender Relations among Ethiopian Immigrant Couples in Toronto." Accessed April 4, 2010. http://ceris.metropolis.net/Virtual%20Library/EResources/Hymanl_et_al_Phase12004.pdf.

Hyman, Ilene, Sepali Guruge, and Robin Mason. 2008. "The Impact of Migration on Marital Relationships: A Study of Ethiopian Immigrants in Toronto." *Journal of Comparative Family Studies* 39(2): 140-163.

Ibieta, Gabriella. 2001. Fragmented Memories: An Exile's Return. In Remembering Cuba: Legacy of a Diaspora, edited by Andrea Herrare, 69-78. Austin: University of Texas Press.

Igwe, Leo. 2009. Caste Discrimination in Africa. International Humanist and Ethical Union. Accessed July 20, 2012. http://www.iheu.org/caste-discrimination-africa.

Jacobson Matthew Frye. 1998. *Whiteness of a Different Color: European Immigrants and the Alchemy of Race.* Cambridge, MA: Harvard University Press.

Jillson, Cal. 2004. *Pursuing the American Dream: Opportunity and Exclusion Over Four Centuries.* Lawrence: University Press of Kansas.

Jischke, Martin. 2007. "The American Dream: What is it? Who is it?" *Vital Speeches of the Day:* 73 (7): 314-315.

Kadianaki, Irini. 2010. "Making Sense of Immigrant Identity Dialogues." *Culture and Psychology* 16(3): 473-448.

Keller, G. 2001. "The New Demographics of Higher Education." *The Review of Higher Education* 24(3): 219-235.

King, Russell. (2000). "Generalizations from the History of Return Migration," in *Return Migration: Journey of Hope or Despair?*, edited by Bimal Ghosh, 7-55. Geneva: International Organization for Migration.

Kposowa, Augustine J. 2002. "Human Capital and the Performance of African Immigrants in the U.S. Labor Market." *The Western Journal of Black Studies* 26: 175-183.

Lee, Everett S. 1966. "A Theory of Migration." *Demography* 3: 47-57.

———. 2004. "Salsa and Ketchup: Transnational Migrants Straddle Two Worlds." *Contexts* 3(2): 20–6.

Levitt, Peggy. 2001. *The Transnational Villagers.* Berkeley: University of California Press.

Lijtmaer, Ruth. 2001. "Splitting and nostalgia in recent immigrants: Psychodynamic Considerations." *Journal of American Academy of Psychoanalysis* 29(3): 427-438.

Lima, Alvaro. 2010. Transnationalism: "A New Mode of Immigrant Integration." The Mauricio Gaston Institute for Latino Community Development and Public Policy, University of Massachusetts. Accessed February 20, 2012 at: http://www.bostonredevelopmentauthority.org/PDF/ResearchPublications/TransnationalismGaston2010.pdf.

Madrigal, Candy. R., and Nazneen Mayadas. 2006. "Push and Pull Factors: A Profile of Colombian Migration to the United States." *Social Development Issues* 28(3): 30-42.

Mahler, Sarah. J. 1995. *American Dreaming: Immigrant Life on the Margins.* Princeton: Princeton University Press.

———. 1999. "Engendering Transnational Migration: A Case Study of Salvadorans."*American Behavioral Scientist* 42: 690-719.

———. 2000. Migration and Transnational Issues: Recent Trends and Prospects for 2020. Hamburg: Institut für Iberoamerika-Kunde, Working Paper # 4. Accessed June 20, 2012.

http://www.grupochorlavi.org/webchorlavi/migraciones2006/bibliografia/Bilio-graf%C3%ADDa%20General/Sarah%20Mahler,%20transnationalism.pdf.

Massey, Douglas. 1999. "Why Does Immigration Occur? A Theoretical Synthesis." In *The Handbook of International Migration, The American Experience*, edited by Charles Hirsch-man, Philip Kasinitz, and Josh DeWind, 34-52. New York: Russell Sage Foundation.

Massey, Douglas, Joaquin Arango, Graeme Hugo, Ali Kouaouci, Adela Pellegrino, and Ed-ward J. Taylor. 1993. "Theories of International Migration: A Review and Appraisal." *Population and Development Review* 19(3): 431-466.

Mason, Patrick, and Austin Algernon. 2011. "The Low Wages of Black Immigrants: Wage Penalties for US-born and Foreign-born Workers". The Economic Policy Institute Briefing Paper # 298. Accessed on July 18, 2012. http://www.epi.org/page//BriefingPa-per298.pdf?nocdn=1.

Mather, Mark. 2009. "Reports on America: Children in Immigrant Families Chart New Path." *Population Reference Bureau*, 1-15.

Mavroudi, Elizabeth. 2010. "Nationalism, the Nation and Migration: Searching for Purity and Diversity." Space and Polity 14(3): 219-233.

Maykut, Pamela, and Richard Morehouse. 1994. *Beginning Qualitative Researchers: A Philo-sophical and Practical Guide*. Washington: Falmer Press.

McCabe, Kristen. 2009. "African Immigrants in the United States." Migration Policy Institute. Accessed June 08, 2011. http://www.migrationinformation.org/feature/display.cfm?ID=847.

McClelland, Peter, and Peter Tobin. 2010. *American Dream Dying: The Challenging Lot of the Least Advantaged*. New York: Rowman & Littlefield Publishers.

McConahay, John. 1986. "Modern Racism, Ambivalence, and Modern Racism Scale." In *Prej-udice, Discrimination, and Racism*, edited by John Dovidio and Samuel Gaertner, 91-125. Orlando: Academic Press.

McConahay, John, Betty Hardee, and Valerie Batts. 1981. "Has Racism Declined? It Depends on Who is Asking and What is Asked." *Journal of Conflict Resolution* 25 (4):563-579.

McDermott, M., and F. L. Samson. 2005. "White Racial and Ethnic Identity in the United States." *Annual Review of Sociology* 31: 245-261.

McKay, Ramah. 2003. "U.S. in Focus: Family Reunification." Migration Policy Institute. Ac-cessed November 15, 2010. http://www.migrationinformation.org/usfocus/dis-play.cfm?id=122.

McNamee, Stephen, and Robert Miller. 2004. *The Meritocratic Myth*. Lanham: Rowman and Littlefield.

McWilliams, Carey. 1973. *Southern California: An Island on the Land*. Santa Barbara, CA: Peregrine Smith.

Miele, Stefano. 1920. "America as a Place to Make Money." *World's Work* 41: 204.

Model, Suzanne. 1997. "An Occupational Tale of Two Cities: Minorities in London and New York." *Demography* 34: 539-550.

Model, Suzanne, and David Lapido. 1996. "Context and Opportunity: Minorities in London and New York." *Social Forces* 75: 485-510.

Moore, Ami R., and Foster K. Amey. 2002. "Earnings Differentials among Male African Immigrants in the United States." *Equal Opportunities International* 21(8): 30-50.

Moore, Ami R., Foster K. Amey, and Yawo Bessa. 2009. "Earnings Attainment of Immigrants in the U.S.: The Effects of Race, Gender, and Place of Birth." *Equal Opportunity Interna-tional* 28(6): 500-512.

Nagel, J. 1994. "Constructing Ethnicity: Creating and Recreating Ethnic Identity and Culture." *Social Problem* 41(1): 152-176.

N'Diaye, Diana Baird and N'Diaye, Gorgui. 2007. "Creating the Vertical Village: Senegalese Traditions of Immigration and Transnational Cultural Life." In Kwadwo Konadu-Agye-mang, Baffour, Takyi, and John A. Arthur (eds). *The New African Diaspora in North America: Trends, Community Building and Adaptation*. Lanham, MD: Lexington Books.

Nyamwange, Monica K., Thomas Owusu, and Philip Thiuri. 2001. "Analysis of Selected Geographical Aspects of Kenyan Immigrants in the United States." *Middle States Geogra-pher* 34: 63-72.

Obiakor, Festus E., and Patrick A. Grant. 2002. *Foreign-born African Americans: Silenced Voices in the Discourse on Race.* New York: Nova Science Publishers.

O'Connor, Julia, Ann Orloff, and Sheila Shaver. 1999. *States, Markets, Families, Gender, Liberalism, and Social Policy in Australia, Canada, Great Britain, and the United States.* Cambridge: Cambridge University Press.

Odera, Lilian A. 2007. "Acculturation, Coping Styles, and Mental Health of First Generation Kenyan Immigrants in the United States." PhD dissertation, University of Michigan.

Ogbaa, Kalu. 2003. *The Nigerian Americans.* Westport: Greenwood Press.

Oliver, Ivan. 1983. "The 'Old' and the 'New' Hermeneutic in Sociological Theory." *The British Journal of Sociology* 34(4): 519-553.

Ong, A. D., Phinney, J. S., and Dennis, J. (2006). "Competence Under Challenge: Exploring the Protective Influence of Parental Support and Ethnic Identity in Latino College Students." *Journal of Adolescence* 29: 961-979.

Orowolo, Oladele, O. 2000. "Return migration and the problem of reintegration." *International Migration* 38(5): 59-82.

Park, Robert. 1928. "Human Migration and the Marginal Man." *The American Journal of Sociology* 33(6): 881-893.

Parrillo, Vincent. 2009. *Strangers to These Shores: Race and Ethnic Relations to the United States,* 9th ed. Boston: Allyn & Bacon.

Patterson, Orlando. 2000. "Taking Culture Seriously: A Framework and an Afro-American Illustration." In *Culture Matters: How Values Shape Human Progress,* edited by Harrison E. Lawrence, and Samuel P. Huntington, 202-218. New York: Basic Books.

Peil, Margaret. 1995. "Ghanaians Abroad." *African Affairs* 94(376): 345-367.

Pessar, Patricia. 1995. *A Visa for a Dream: Dominicans in the United States.* Boston: Allyn and Bacon.

Phinney, Jean, Cyndy Cantu and Dawn Kurtz 1997. "Ethnic and American Identity as Predictors of Self-esteem among African American, Latino, and White adolescents." *Journal of Youth and Adolescence* 26: 165-185.

Phinney, Jean, Horenczyk, Gabriel, Liebkind, Karmela, and Paul Vedder. 2001. "Ethnic Identity, Immigration, and Well-being: An Interactional Perspective." *Journal of Social Issues* 57(3): 493-510.

Phinney, Jean, Romero, Irma, Nava, Monica, and Dan Huang. 2001. "The Role of Language, Parents, and Peers in Ethnic Identity among Adolescents in Immigrant Families." *Journal of Youth and Adolescence* 30(2): 135-153.

Picca, Leslie H., and Joe R. Feagin. 2007. *Two-faced Racism: Whites in the Backstage and Frontstage.* New York: Routledge/Taylor & Francis Group.

Platteau, Jean-Philippe. 1996. "Physical Infrastructure as a Constraint on Agricultural Growth: The Case of sub-Saharan Africa." *Oxford Development Studies* 24 (3): 189-219.

Porter, Gina. 2002. "Living in a Walking World: Rural Mobility and Social Equity Issues in sub-Saharan Africa." *World Development* 30(2): 285-300.

Portes, Alejandro, Guarnizo, Luis, and Patricia Landolt. 1999. "The Study of Transnationalism: Pitfalls and Promise of an Emergent Research Field." *Ethnic and Racial Studies* 22 (2): 217-236.

Portes, Alejandro and Rubén Rumbaut. 2006. *Immigrant America.* Berkeley: University of California Press.

Portes, Alejandro, and Min Zhou. 1993. "The New Second Generation: Segmented Assimilation and its Variants." *Annals of the American Academy of Political and Social Science* 530: 74-96.

Poston, Dudley L. 1994. "Patterns of Economic Attainment of Foreign-born Male Workers in the United States." *International Migration Review* 28: 478-500.

Public Law 89-236—Oct3. 1965. "To Amend the Immigration and Nationality Act, and for Other Purposes." Accessed May 8, 2011. http://library.uwb.edu/guides/USimmigration/79%20stat%20911.pdf.

Quintana, S. M. (2007). "Racial and Ethnic Identity: Developmental perspectives and research." *Journal of Counseling Psychology* 54: 259-270.

Rattansi, Ali. 2007. *Racism: A Very Short Introduction.* Oxford: Oxford University Press.

Ravenstein, G. Ernest. 1885. "The Laws of Migration." *Journal of the Royal Statistical Society* 48: 167-227.

———. 1889. "The Laws of Migration." *Journal of the Royal Statistical Society* 52: 214-301.

Reagan, Patricia B., and Randall J. Olsen. 2000. "You Can Go Home Again: Evidence from Longitudinal Data." *Demography* 37(3): 239-350.

Reed, Holly E., and Catherine S. Andrzejewski. 2010. "The New Wave of African Immigrants in the United States." A Paper presented at the 2010 Population Association of America Annual Meeting: Dallas, Texas. Accessed June 11, 2011. http://paa2010.princeton.edu/download.aspx?submissionId=100606.

Reimers, M. David. 1992. *Still the Golden Door: The Third World Comes to America* . New York: Columbia University Press.

Richardson, Alan. 1968. "A Shipboard Study of Some British Born Immigrants Returning to the United Kingdom from Australia." *International Migration* 6:221-238.

Schor, Juliet. 1992. *The Overworked American: The Unexpected Decline of Leisure.* New York: Harper Collins.

Shafer, E. Byron. 1999. "American Exceptionalism." *Annual Review of Political Science* 2: 445-463.

Sinatti, G. 2011. "'Mobile Transmigrants' or 'Unsettled Returnees'? Myth of Return and Permanent Resettlement among Senegalese migrants." *Population, Space and Place*, 17: 153-166.

Sladkova, Jana. 2007. "Expectations and Motivations of Hondurans Migrating to the United States." *Journal of Community & Applied Social Psychology* 17: 187-202.

Smith, Estellie. M. 1980. "The Portuguese Female Immigrant: The 'Marginal Man.' *International Migration Review* 14(1): 77-92.

Sowell, Thomas. 1981. *Ethnic America: A History.* New York: Basic Books.

Stepick, Alex, and Carol Dutton Stepick. 2009. "Diverse Contexts of Reception and Feelings of Belonging." *Forum: Qualitative Social Research* 10(3) Art: 15.

Sudarkasa, N. (1981). "Interpreting the African Heritage in Afro-American Family Organization." In *Black Families,* edited by H. P. McAdoo, 37-53. Beverly Hills, CA: Sage.

Sunil, Thankam, Rojas, Viviana, and Bradley, Don. 2007. "United States' International Retirement Migration: The Reasons for Retiring to the Environs of Lake Chapala, Mexico." *Ageing and Society*, 27: 489-510.

Taylor, D. Garth, Paul Sheatsley, and Andrew Greeley. 1978. "Attitudes Toward Racial Integration." *Scientific American* 238:42-49.

Taylor, Steven J., and Robert Bogdan. 1998. *Introduction to Qualitative Research Methods: A Guidebook and Resource,* 3rd ed. New York: John Wiley & Sons.

Teferra, Damtow, and Philip Albachi. 2004. "African Higher Education: Challenges for the 21st Century." *Higher Education* 47(1):21-50.

Teo, Sin Yih. 2011. "The Moon Back Home is Brighter?: Return Migration and Cultural Politics of Belonging. *Journal of Ethnic and Migration Studies* 37(5): 805-820.

Terrazas, Aaron. 2009. "African Immigrants in the United States." Accessed November 07, 2009. http://www.migrationinformation.org/USFocus/print.cfm?ID=719.

Thomas, David. 2001. "The Truth about Mentoring Minorities: Race Matters." *Harvard Business Review* 79(4): 98-107.

Todaro, Michael. 1969. "A Model of Labor Migration and Urban Unemployment in Less Developed Countries." *American Economic Review* 59(1): 138–48.

Todaro, Michael, and Lydia Maruszko. 1987. "Illegal Migration and US Immigration Reform: A Conceptual Framework." *Population and Development Review* 13: 101-114.

Toren, Nina. 1979. Return to Zion: "Characteristics and Motivations of Returning Emigrants." *Social Forces* 54(3): 546-558.

Trueba, Henry. 2002. "Multiple Ethnic, Racial, and Cultural Identities in Action: From Marginality to a New Cultural Capital in Modern Society." *Journal of Latinos and Education* 1(1): 7-28.

Tummala-Narra, Pratyusha. 2009. "The Immigrant's Real and Imagined Return Home." *Psychoanalysis, Culture and Society* 14(3): 237-252.

United Nations. 2002. United Nations International Migration Report. Accessed November 04, 2011. http://www.brookings.edu/events/2003/0212global-governance.aspx?p=1.
U.S. Department of State. 2010. *Diplomacy in Action*. Accessed March 30, 2011. http://www.state.gov/r/pa/ei/bgn/2860.htm.
———. 2011. *Diplomacy in Action*. Accessed March 30, 2011. http://www.state.gov/r/pa/ei/bgn/2859.htm.
van Ecke, Yolanda. 2005. "Immigration From an Attachment Perspective." *Social Behavior and Personality* 467-476.
Verkuyten, M. and A. de Wolf. 2002. "Being, Feeling and Doing: Discourses and Ethnic Self-Definitions among Minority Group Members." *Culture and Psychology* 8: 371-399.
Vertovec, Steven. 2001. "Transnationalism and Identity." *Journal of Ethnic and Migration Studies* 27(4): 573-582.
———. 2004. "Trends and Impacts of Migrant Transnationalism." Center on Migration, Policy and Society, Working Paper number 03. Oxford: University of Oxford.
Waldinger, Roger, and David Fitzgerald. 2004. "Transnationalism in Questions." *American Journal of Sociology* 109(5):1177-1195.
Waters, Mary C. 1990. *Ethnic Options: Choosing Identities in America*. Berkeley: University of California Press.
———. 1994. "Ethnic and Racial Identities of Second Generation Black Immigrants in New York City." *International Migration Review* 28(4): 795-820.
Waters, Mary C., and Tomás R. Jiménez. 2005. "Assessing Immigrant Assimilation: New Empirical and Theoretical Challenges." *Annual Review of Sociology* 31: 105-125.
Weisberger, Adam. 1992. "Marginality and its Directions." *Sociological Forum* 7(5): 425-446.
Willie, Charles V. 1989. *Caste and Class Controversy*, 2nd ed. New York: Rowman & Littlefield.
Wilson, William J. 1980. *The Declining Significance of Race*, 2nd ed. Chicago: University of Chicago Press.
———. 2009. *More Than Just Race: Being Black and Poor in the Inner City*. New York: Norton & Company.
Wong, C. A., Eccles, J. S., and Sameroff, A. (2003). "The Influence of Ethnic Discrimination and Ethnic Identification on African American Adolescents' School and Socioemotional Adjustment." *Journal of Personality* 71: 1197–1232.
The World Bank. 2010. Financing higher education in Africa. Accessed December 28, 2011. http://siteresources.worldbank.org/EDUCATION/Resources/2782001099079877269/Financing_higher_edu_Africa.pdf.
Yeboah, Ian E. A. 2008. *Black African Neo-diaspora: Ghanaian Immigrant Experiences in the Greater Cincinnati, Ohio, Area*. New York: Lexington Books.
Zeng, Zhen, and Yu Xie. 2004. "Asian-American's Earnings Disadvantage Reexamined: The Role of Place of Education." *American Journal of Sociology* 5: 1075-1108.
Zhou, Min. 1997. "Segmented Assimilation: Issues, Controversies, and Recent Research on the New Second Generation." *International Migration Review* 31(4): 975-1008.

Index

Abasi (study respondent), 19, 34, 69
Abeba (study respondent), 31, 56, 75–76
academic achievement, 38
Adams, James Truslow, 1, 10, 23, 27, 43, 63, 89–90
Afaafa (study respondent), 20, 84
Afolabi (study respondent), 33–34
Afrocentrism, 83
Agatha (study respondent), 22, 72–73
Akim (study respondent), 46, 76
Akosua (study respondent), 24
Akthar (study respondent), 50
Alfred (study respondent), 75
American Dream: achievement perceptions, 36; and betterment of self, 48–50; definitions of, 1–2, 4, 10, 27, 29–32, 32–36, 63; and fulfillment, 45–48, 54–56; immigrants' definition of, 27–41; and incomplete lives of immigrants, 50–53; and opportunity, 56–58; origin of idea, 28; and social equity, 58–63
Anglo-culture, 68
Anglophone students, 16
Anglos, 2
Anita (study respondent), 36–37, 59–60
Anthony (study respondent), 57, 60–61, 63
Aranda, Elizabeth, 73
assimilation, 3

background of study subjects, 7–9

Bandele (study respondent), 57
Beheilu (study respondent), 29–30, 84–85
Benjamin, Lois, 53
Black Chamber of Commerce, 62
The Black Elite (Benjamin), 53
Bourdieu, Pierre, 10, 45
bribery, 46
Brint, Steven, 32
Brodwin, Paul, 80
burial practices, 71–72
business ownership, 39, 61–62

Canada, 61
career goals, 38, 53
Carlos (study respondent), 53, 55, 68, 72, 82–83
caste-based discrimination, 63
Celine (study respondent), 31, 70
Cerase, Francesco P., 65, 72, 77
Charles (study respondent), 40, 49, 87
children of immigrants: and cultural identity, 44; and ethnic identity, 11, 79, 80–81, 83–85, 87; obstacles faced by, 90; opportunities available to, 24; prospects for, 86–87, 87–88; social marginalization of, 79–80, 81–83
citizenship, 6, 79, 86
civil rights movement, 28, 45
civil war, 9, 17
Clara (study respondent), 34
class issues, 2–3, 51–52

collective identity, 80
colonial rule, 7, 9
communication technology, 18, 67
competition, 40, 61
conservatism, 65
consumerism, 24, 90. *See also* material
    wealth
corruption, 46
cost of living, 11, 70
country of origin quotas, 13
credit, 57
Crevecoeur, Hector St. John de, 10, 28–29,
    33–34, 41
crime, 46
cultural backgrounds: and achievement of
    the American Dream, 37; and
    assimilation of immigrants, 3; and
    children of immigrants, 24, 82, 83;
    difficulties of new immigrants, 24; and
    immigrants' expectations of the United
    States, 20, 21; and modern racism, 59;
    and return migration, 68, 69, 71–72;
    and social structure of the United
    States, 46; and struggles of immigrants,
    43–44. *See also* ethnic identity

Darweshi (study respondent), 33, 75
data collection, 4–5
Dawit (study respondent), 20–21, 50–51,
    81–82
De Haas, Hein, 14
death, 71–72
Declaration of Independence, 28
democracy, 32
demographics: of Ethiopia, 7; of Ghana, 8;
    and immigration quotas, 13; of Kenya,
    9; of Nigeria, 9
diasporic groups, 80
discrimination: in American business
    relations, 60–61, 62; caste-based, 63;
    and children of immigrants, 81, 85; and
    incomplete life of immigrants, 53; in
    Kenya, 62–63; and meritocracy, 57; and
    obstacles faced by immigrants, 40, 53;
    and prospects for immigrants, 91,
    91–92, 92–93; and return migration, 91,
    92; strategies to overcome, 63; and
    work ethic, 62

diversity: among immigrants, 2; of
    Ethiopia, 7; of Ghana, 8; of Kenya, 9;
    of Nigeria, 9; and race relations in the
    U.S., 59. *See also* ethnic identity
Doja, Mrs. (study respondent), 16, 33, 34,
    62, 71
domestic labor, 20, 49
dreams of immigrants, 18
duration of immigrant residence, 89

economics: and cost of living, 11; and
    immigrants' definition of the American
    Dream, 27; and immigration policy, 7;
    and neoclassical theory, 14–15; and
    opportunity available to immigrants,
    22; push-and-pull factors in
    immigration, 14–15, 16; and reasons to
    immigrate, 2–3, 24; and return
    migration, 65–66, 70, 74, 92
Edem (study respondent), 34
Education: and achievement of the
    American Dream, 36; and children of
    immigrants, 87; and decisions to
    migrate, 90; and definition of the
    American Dream, 31, 31–32; in
    Ethiopia, 7; and fulfillment of
    immigrants' goals, 54; in Ghana, 8, 49;
    and goals of the American Dream,
    37–38, 38–39; and immigrants' views
    of the United States, 19; and incomplete
    life of immigrants, 52, 53; and obstacles
    faced by immigrants, 63; and
    opportunities available to immigrants,
    22, 24; and prospects for immigrants,
    89, 90, 91–92; push-and-pull factors in
    immigration, 15–16; and reasons to
    immigrate, 2; and return migration, 73;
    and study sample, 6; and subject
    selection criteria, 6; tracking in, 31, 32
Edward (study respondent), 17
Emmanuel (study respondent), 22
employment, 63, 73
entrepreneurship, 39, 40
The Epic of America (Adams), 1, 43
Ethiopia: background information, 7; and
    children of immigrants, 81, 81, 82,
    84–85, 88; civil war, 17; ethnic
    identification of immigrants, 11; and
    immigrants' views of the United States,